MOM
of
TWO

Catalina Tagarta

Parenting tips for raising healthy and confident children

MOM
of
TWO

Study case:
Erik and gluten-free life at 3 years old

Catalina Tagarta

Author: Catalina Tagarta
Proofreading: Maria Simona Banulescu
Technoediting: Catalina Tagarta
Graphic Design Tool: Canva.com

@ 2022 Author

E-mail: contact.tagarta@gmail.com

SITECH Publishing House is part of the list of Romanian publishing houses accredited by CNSIS and is also part of the list of publishing houses with prestige recognized by CNCS, through CNATDCU, for Panel 4.

ISBN: 978-606-45-1449-3

DEDICATION

To my firstborn son, who needs to be on a permanent diet.

To families all around the world who struggle to raise healthy, confident children, with or without health problems.

Mom of Two

CONTENTS

ACKNOWLEDGMENTS

First of all I thank to my husband, who supports me in everything and reminds me every time I can't that "I can do a bit more", he has facilitated the writing process during the time he spent with the children.

I also thank to:

- Dr Gabriela Bar - primary paediatric doctor and head of department of the National Institute for Mother and Child Health "Alessandrescu-Rusescu", who made the necessary investigations to establish the diagnosis, after many other visits to various doctors,

- Dr Lidia Cremer, PhD, scientific researcher, trainer and nutrition consultant, who responded positively to my invitation for medical advice in order to provide accurate information,

- My mother, who taught me the true values of life, who lovingly educated me and gave us all a lesson of life by beating cancer with her optimistic way of "just being",

- To my children's paternal grandparents, who are extraordinary people, to my sister and brother-in-law, who took their role as gluten-free cooks seriously.

- Mirela-Carmen Stancu, book & life coach, without whose guidance I would not have had the courage to publish so quickly.

- To the friends who are close to me and to my mentors, who constantly give me valuable advice.

FOREWARD

I first met Catalina Tagarta on a late spring day when, in a telegraphic style, she announced that she wanted to write "a book... for children". We were organizing, at that time, the 12th edition of the course on how to structure a nonfiction book. As such, the three points included in the presentation were by no means extra.

I have to admit, I was initially left in a state of stupefaction (or as the saying goes, open-mouthed). And if you're wondering what the reason was, I can assure you that, most of the time, a children's book doesn't fall into the nonfiction category. I could even imagine myself struggling to explain to the future author that she wasn't on the right course. However, it wasn't long before I realized that her "desire" was perfect for nonfiction.

And just like that, we rolled up our sleeves to begin work on the structure of her upcoming book, **"Mom of Two"**.

The book that... you're now holding in your hands.

The book that... will win the hearts of children who are gluten intolerant and sensitive to any contamination, bring relief to parents facing these issues and reveal solutions... many... to anyone who wants to understand and help the loved ones in similar situations.

A book that... could have, successfully, fallen into the "3-in-1" category. Your favorite flavor is your choice.

Also, my part in this book (quite minor) is strictly related to the structure and planning section but... all credit goes to the author. Both for the impactful book she has written, a book that has the potential to change the lives of those facing the same frustrations for the better, and for the passion and sustained pace she has infused into the book writing process.

I could go on and on about the subject... that is the admiration I had for the author from the very first moment. I could even demonstrate how useful and how profound the words used in the book are.

But... I choose to end my short presentation with the same words Catalina said when I asked her why she wanted to write a book. This book:

"... to help as many children with food allergies and intolerances as possible to better understand their condition and provide them with a greater degree of comfort once they realize they are not the only freaks on the planet. It was and still is very, very hard for me to explain to my child why he is not allowed to eat certain things. It would have helped if there was a book like this. And I thought I should write it myself. Although there were other topics on my list before :) at least 2 memoirs... "

And that being said, I invite you with the greatest love to enjoy the words from this book and reveal its wisdom.

And I... I am waiting for "the two memoirs". With hope and anticipation.

Mirela-Carmen Stancu, book & life coach
January 11th 2022, Bucharest

FROM THE AUTHOR

The book started as a sort of play in the evenings. Tired after the challenges of the day and the many refusals to let him eat bread, bagels, biscuits or any other gluten-containing bakery product that we encountered on every street corner, I started making up stories. I couldn't come up with a more brilliant idea to better explain to my child, almost 3 years old at the time, why he suddenly wasn't allowed to eat like he used to. I've been reading to him since he was little and he's passionate about stories. We could have used a book in which we discovered a character going through what was happening to him, but since we couldn't find one, we made one up ourselves. And to help him identify with the character, we even named him Eric, with a "C". And he began to fall in love with his new tiz. In the evening, after we finished reading the bedtime story, because he still couldn't fall asleep and kept asking me all sorts of questions like "Why, until when?" we kept telling the story for about an hour. Every evening he raised new questions for me, I learned new things about him, which brought us closer to each other and helped us understand him, support him and protect him more and more. Our conversations are often memorable, taking us from laughing to crying, from play to meditation and back again. So I began to put some of it down on paper and outline the story as I would have liked to read it from someone else. Maybe it would have helped us get through the whole story more easily and accept reality more quickly.

It's not a magic recipe or an example to follow, it's simply the journey of a normal experience, the story of people learning from mistakes, researching and growing day by day, trying to turn the gluten-free diet into a healthy lifestyle. And, in the end, become the best version of themselves.

1. SOMETHING'S WRONG

*

Erik is a big boy. He's settled into the idea of going to nursery, he's even made friends with his classmates and has favourites among the teaching ladies. He is enthusiastic about the children, playing with them and discovering everything around him. He speaks almost correctly and a lot. He is curious by nature and there is no shortage of pranks in his daily schedule. But for a while now, unfortunately, the tummy pains have not been absent from the evening programme.

"Mommy, is my milk ready?"

"In a moment", replied Mommy.

"Come on, make it quick!"

"My dear, you must learn to be patient", said Mommy gently. "It will only take a few minutes."

The time is slow when you wait for the evening elixir, and there is a big smile on his face as he gets his bottle.

"It's about time you start drinking milk from the cup, unless you want to give it up completely", says Mom.

"But I want my milk from the bottle, please!"

"Only babies drink milk from the bottle."

"But I want it. Please, Mommy, please!"

"Only if you tell me why you like drinking from the bottle so much."

"Because I can drink the milk in peace when I'm lying on my back on the pillow and it doesn't drip on me," the little boy replies seriously. "Look", he says as he sank into the soft pillow. "Unbelievable", says Dad, who was passing by in the hallway and caught their conversation. "Mommy, it seems to me that you've got the most mature answer", he said laughing. "Now you work it out! Dad gave him a goodnight kiss, turned off the light and left to check the little brother, while Erik began drinking his milk hungrily. He has a favourite bottle, the teat of which he has bitten off until it has enlarged its opening, so that the liquid flows quickly and the bottle empties immediately. Nestled next to him, mom gently strokes his leg, his arm, his

back, to help him fall asleep faster. He loves to be massaged and comforted. Suddenly, however, the child sits up and cries out loud, as if he's had a fantastic idea, just before he falls asleep:
"I want a banana!"
"It's 10 o'clock at night. Dinner has finished long ago, you've already had your evening milk, it's time for bed", says the mother.
"I want a banana!" cried Erik, to the exasperation of his mother, who prayed that their noise would not wake up the baby sleeping the next room.
"Calm down, please! Tomorrow for snack, or even for breakfast, if you really care, you'll get bananas. But now it's late, it's time to sleep."
"I want a banana", Erik cries again, and starts rolling around in bed.
His mother is not impressed by his "performance". The scenario repeats itself night after night, so she wonders, for the hundredth time, if she's doing something wrong. Either he doesn't eat enough in terms of quality or quantity at dinner in the evening, or it's not the right time for dinner, or his stomach digests food too quickly, or he gets tired of the bath and wants more to eat afterwards, or maybe it's the milk, he gets hungry for milk... Anyway, the point is, no matter how he does it, whether she gives him bananas or not, the outcome is the same. Soon, the message that has been tormenting her for some time, that has put her on pause and haunts her nights comes:
"Mommy, my tummy hurts!" says Erik soon, his voice torn with pain and dripping with sleep.
"Oh, my God! What are we going to do with these tummy aches", complains Mom.
"I don't know!" replied the child, like a big, wise man. "Mommy, it hurts so much."
The mother's face is completely blank. She feels lost, misunderstood, disoriented. Maybe today she could have avoided the pain if she had given him a banana!
"What are we going to do with this pain?" the child repeats, following her mother, who is wandering around the house in

search of some solution. The candlelight they use at night during sleep no longer helps her. Tension rises and she turns on the light bulb.

Lying on the living room carpet, the tiny, frail body of the little boy is shaking with pain.

The mother struggles to keep herself from crying, from agitating him too. The father hears the alarm and slowly walks out of the bedroom, in order not to wake the little boy.

"We can't go on like this! It's not normal for him to have such a swollen tummy if he has nothing" the mother says.

"Possibly. But what can we do? The doctor said he looks fine, he's okay."

"Mommy, it hurts so much... Rub my tummy again, please!"

"I'll get another opinion! We gave up cow's milk a long time ago, we eat as healthy as we can, but his tummy is still swollen and painful", says Mom. "Tomorrow I will schedule him somewhere else."

"Shall we go to the doctor to give me syrup, so my tummy will feel better?" asks the boy.

"Yes, my baby. We're going to get you some syrup. We'll be fine, baby! Let's just calm down. Mommy's here. Everything's gonna be all right. Come on, close your eyes. Try and get some rest!"

"Mommy, will you tell me the story of Eric, the little boy whose tummy always hurts?" the baby asks in a sleepy voice.

"Yes, my dear! There was once a little boy, Eric, who was almost three years old. He was loved by his parents, grandparents, uncles and aunts, friends, everyone... He was a very smart and brave child. When he needed to go to the doctor, the little boy knew that the gentlemen and ladies in white coats were doctors or nurses who only wanted to do him well. Sometimes, they just need to listen to his chest and look in his neck or tummy, other times they might even have to prick him, take a little blood, to do a set of tests, from which they will be able to detect why his tummy always hurts, especially in the evenings after he drinks his milk. It's possible that when they take his blood with a very thin needle, his arm will hurt a little, but he doesn't cry too much, because afterwards he has to tell his little brother how brave he was. Eric loves him very much, and although he doesn't always give him all his toys when his little one wants them, he defends him from all the strangers in the park who want to touch him telling them: 'Don't touch him! He is little, and then he can stick his hands in his mouth and get sick.' Eric is also a wonderful little boy, because he understands that babies need a lot of attention from their parents, and he tries not to get too upset when mom is breastfeeding his little one, because he knows she will spend enough time with him afterwards..." finishes the mother, when she sees that the little boy has calmed down and finally managed to fall asleep. She wraps him up lovingly and stays snuggled next to him.

Ever since he was one, Erik has slept alone in his room. But now his mother can't bear to let him go. She feels him fragile and helpless, and his voice echoes in her mind over and over again: 'Mommy, I want to sleep with you.' He says: "to sleep", not "to fall asleep", so the mother stays by his side until the baby wakes up for the first time.

**

"Good morning, sleepyhead!" whispers his mother as she puts his socks on.

"Where are we going?"

"Where? To the nursery. The ladies are waiting for you, the children... But tell me: how's your tummy today?"

"It's fine!"

Mom is satisfied with the answer and continues dressing. It's easier this way, when he's half asleep. Otherwise, he gets ideas that he'd like to stay at home with Dodo, laze around, play with something or watch cartoons.

"Come on, sleepyhead!" Mommy picks him up, gives him a little hug and they go to the bathroom together to wash his face and teeth.

"I don't want to go!" cries Erik, as if he has only just realised that he is caught in the middle of a conspiracy. "When are the two days I'm staying home? Aren't they yesterday?"

Mother laughs heartily.

"Are you laughing at me?" said the little boy, emphasizing the appellation.

"My dear, I explained to you that yesterday is what it was, so the day before, today is what we are living now, here, and tomorrow is the next day, so the day to come. And we are still far away until our two days off. Today is only Tuesday, and the days off are Saturday and Sunday. It would be good to repeat the days of the week when you come from nursery, what do you think? We also have an interesting book on the subject, remember? Anyway, let's have a quick recap: the week has 7 days. So, 5 fingers on one hand and 2 on the other. The first 5 are usually working days: Monday, Tuesday, Wednesday, Thursday, Friday, which is usually a shorter day, most people don't have long hours at work, and the other 2 weekend days, which are also called weekends, are Saturday and Sunday. Remember? So, how many days until the weekend?"

"So many", Erik points with his little fingers.

"Good job! Three days. If today is only Tuesday, we still have Wednesday, Thursday and Friday. Then you'll be home for two days. What would you like to do on your days off?"

"Let's go to Grandma's."

"All right. But... if we were to stay at home, what activities would you like to do after us adults finish our chores?"

"Play!"

"I'm sure you would like it. I was just curious... what would that involve?"

"Like what, Mommy? Toys, of course", said the child enthusiastically, managing to get a smile out of Mom again.

"Come on, no more talk! Either brush your teeth or get your shoes on quickly, we're both going to be late", called Daddy, who was waiting at the door. "If you're good, I'll take you to the horses this weekend."

"Yes, I will be good!", Erik shouted happily. "I want to go riding, Daddy." Father won him over with a grand promise and they set off up the stairs together, leaving Mother with the same thought in her mind: 'Where should the search for further investigation begin? Because his doctor said the baby was fine, he looked perfect.'

2. AT THE DOCTOR: EXAMINATION AND INVESTIGATIONS

It has been said that when you strongly believe in something, or when you really want something and you release your wish into the Universe by saying it, the Universe works in your favour. The same happened in this situation. Erik's mother asked a lot of people for doctors with expertise in digestive problems or for general practitioners with expertise. She finally received a referral to a very dedicated doctor who was willing to further investigate the child's tummy aches. But every moment spent in the waiting room was well worth it.

"Tomorrow we'll go to the doctor to take another look at your tummy", Erik's mother told him one day.

"To see if he'll give me some syrups so I feel no more pain?" the child asked.

"Yes" answered the mother. "But please don't get scared and cry like you did last time we went for the abdominal ultrasound. You were so scared then, that the doctor didn't get to examine you very well. If you don't stay calm, they can't do your investigations properly. Please!"

"Okay, Mommy."

"Will you at least try to stay calm? He'll just look at your belly and put his hand on it like I'm doing now. Same with the ultrasound. I explained you it's a little cold, but it doesn't hurt. If there's a swollen belly, it really doesn't show much. It might hurt a little when they take your tests."

"Yeah. But just a little, okay?"

"I'm not gonna lie to you. You know I've never done this before. I prefer to tell you the truth. It might hurt, but not very much. Depends on how sensitive your body is. If you feel like crying a little, you can! I just ask you to stop when it doesn't hurt anymore, which is right after the needle comes out. Many times, children cry afterwards because of fear, but that crying is no longer from pain. Do you understand? So, it's okay if you cry a little bit, but then you promise to try to calm down, collect your strength and focus your attention on something else, okay? There's no way to avoid the stinging pain, unfortunately. You can just try not to pay attention to the sting, look in the opposite direction, or bite your teeth hardly at that moment, in case it helps. Look, for example when they took Dodo's tests, he didn't cry at all. The nurses were surprised. But it's okay when kids cry, too. Just a little. Okay?"

"Okay!"

The next morning, Dodo stays with Grandma, who arms herself with lots of patience, a baby bottle of tea and a few types of snacks. She wishes good luck to mother and Erik, who go to the doctor in search of a diagnosis. Mom has also armed herself with a few coloured pencils and writing sheets, a little machine and a few other toys to make the waiting time easier. The appointment was late, but Mom enjoyed her precious time with her big boy. They rarely have time for just the two of them.

"Let's draw a hand", says Erik.

"Okay. But then we'll draw a house or an animal or something else?"

"No. Still a little hand." That's his favourite game when he sees a pen and paper. Ever since Mom showed him how to draw the outline of his hand and foot, he's wanted to do just that. He finds it great fun and wants to take his shoes off.

"Let's draw my little foot, Mommy", he said enthusiastically.

"No, my dear. We can't take our shoes off here in the hospital."

"But why not?"

"Because no one takes their shoes off here at all."

"Why not?"

"Because it's not nice."

"Why isn't it nice?"

"Because people come here, do their work and then leave, they don't take their shoes off in the waiting room."

"But why don't people take their shoes off in the waiting room, Mommy?"

"Because the doctor can call them in for their appointment right then and there, and if they're barefoot, they won't be able to walk quickly to the office, and they would miss their turn, and then they have to wait their turn again."

"But why should they wait again?"

"Because someone else comes in instead of them. I think..." said his mother, a little confused.

"And they can't go barefoot? I go to Grandma's yard barefoot, Mommy. Why can't they go like this here?"

"Because there are germs. We can't go barefoot everywhere."

"Why can't we go barefoot everywhere, Mommy?"

"Because..., because then you put your dirty foot in your shoes, and when you get home, you take your shoes off and carry the mess to bed and that's how we get sick, and then we go to the doctor again, and so on, said Mommy, watching how the few people in the waiting room were amused by their endless 'why' conversation.

"Come on, Mommy, please, let's play with the foot one more time! Just once, just once!" Erik continues as he struggles to kick his shoes off. Luckily, the resident arrived to invite them to the much-awaited meeting, and Mom "escaped" from taking off his shoes and arguing.

"What's bothering you, young man? the doctor asked in passing, as she continued to talk passionately to her residents...

"He's swollen in the tummy and he's always complaining that it hurts. The pains were initially occasional, but then they got worse. In the last week he's had a few bad episodes night after night. I don't know what else to do to him and what could be the cause. I've associated it with evening milk, but it's not clear to me if that's the cause.

"What kind of milk does he drink?

"He was breastfed for a long time, but after I stopped breastfeeding for a few months he didn't want milk, then I gently introduced him to goat milk. That's how a doctor advised us it would be better, although tests showed no intolerance to it. And since he discovered goat milk, he always asks for it in the evening.

"What else can you tell us about his history?

"Looking back, I can say that diversification has been a failure. He didn't want to eat anything anymore. Initially we thought he was in tune with the BLW trend, that he wanted chunks instead of pasty, that he had "personality" and wanted to eat on his own, but the truth is we were just lying to ourselves.The reality was that he was not eating. I could have promised him anything, made like the little train, he just wouldn't open his mouth. All he wanted was breast. This was also the reason I ended up weaning him earlier than I would have liked. I don't know if I did right or wrong, but that's how I felt it was ok for both of us at the time.

"Erik, what do you like to eat? the doctor asks.

Erik looks shy and can't articulate a word.

"Mommy, please answer the doctor! Come on, don't be afraid! I told you that you can't talk to strangers in the park. And don't go with them! With people we talk to, and in our presence, it's okay to talk, baby!"

"I don't know if it's just shyness or if he's got this thing about not talking back to people, not talking to them, because I've been warning him not to talk to them and not to go off with strangers. I don't know how well I did it, but when he was a baby, up to a year old and even after that, he was a very happy child, laughing at everyone and very friendly. When I walked with him in the park, anyone would take him by the hand and he would laugh and walk away, waving goodbye, without giving any sign to turn to me. I seriously questioned myself when he reached out his hand to walk away with a homeless man laughing at him, and then I said this is serious what is happening and I have to take action. Anyway... you don't have time for stories like that. Erik, will you show the doctor where it hurts?"

The mother tries to pick him up and put him on the bed so he can be checked, and the little boy starts to cry.

"Don't cry, baby! She's not doing you any harm here. Just take a little look, palpate, like I'm massaging you, okay?"

The doctor examines him quickly, between sobs and struggles, and dictates her verdict to the residents, who then remain to continue the investigation.

"So, does your tummy hurt from the milk?"

"From the bottle maybe", jokes the mother.

"Not from the bottle", says the baby suddenly.

"Look, we'll have to do some investigations, take some blood. You'll be good, right?"

Erik makes a serious face, his eyes become damp like a very scared bunny and he suddenly stands up:

"Let's go", he finally says, very determined.

His mother pretends not to understand:

"Come on, Mommy, let's go!"

"Where shall we go?"

"Home. Come on, let's go home", says the child, as he pulls her hand tightly.

The mother stands immobile, resisting the child's insistence as he pulls her harder and harder.

"Baby, we'll get your tests done first, and then we'll go! We'll be done in a minute. There's no reason to panic. I promise everything will be fine! Come on, please! Look, the kids are sitting quietly in the blood collection chair. The calmer you are, the faster it'll pass and the easier you'll tolerate it."

Erik, however, seemed to have stopped processing the information. His mother's words weren't helping. On the contrary, they seemed to increase his suffering. The child couldn't help himself and began to tear up with sobs. The nurse collected as quickly as she could, because she had a lot of samples to take. At the end, he gave him a little pin for courage and wished him good health. But Erik couldn't hear. He was swollen from crying and was now concentrating on the site of the sting and the patch taped to his arm. He didn't want to take it off until evening, when Dad came home from work. He told him the truth, though, that he had cried a lot, despite the bubble he received for courage. After all, it's a good thing he stayed that way and that they were able to find his vein and prick him the first time. Because when he was younger, he had a nasty experience with... hidden veins and nurses climbing on the baby to prick him.... Probably he got the doctor's fear from that time.

With all her documentation on parenting, personal development and reverse psychology, at this point the mother seems to be overwhelmed by the situation, none of the methods she has learned from courses or books seems to work. She notes, with sadness, that the children's reactions are sometimes so strong that she really doesn't know how to calm them down. Especially when he's tired, if he starts crying, Erik doesn't react to anything. He only has demands and doesn't want to give in under any circumstances, no matter what people may promise him or what they do. Then he wants to sleep with mom, with dad, then with grandma, then he asks for a candy, when he gets one, he wants a second one, then he wants to watch cartoons, eat some pancakes, listen to a story and so on... Do what? What else is he supposed to do? Where am I going wrong? parents wonder helplessly. Erik catches their tender spot and exploits every moment as much as he can until he gets what he wants. He speculates as much as he can, everything.

It's exactly the same today, when he wears the bandage on his hand until late at night. It was with great difficulty that his parents managed to convince him to take it off in the bathroom, explaining that it would get wet anyway, and wouldn't look good on his arm. All things considered; Erik is the family's spoiled kid today. Arriving home only around noon, mother quickly took little Dodo in, who had already had two naps on Grandma's shift, who was very pleased and excited that the baby was no trouble: he had eaten very well and was happy.

3. PLAYING NURSE WITH LITTLE BROTHER

Erik hugs Dodo as if he hasn't seen him since ages:

"Little one, there you are!" he shouts excitedly when he sees him at the door. Dodo laughs out loud when he sees Erik and sits down. Erik gets in front of him and the two of them start walking around the living room. With his mouth up to his ears, Erik talks nonsense, hums a little "It's your birthday" and calls on the little one until he tires him out. Parents and grandparents interfere in their play, as Erik has a tendency to push the little one or climb on him, or get crazy ideas, get him in the pram or grab his legs and pull him just as the baby is getting up from the edge of the bed on his insecure little feet.

"Let him go, little boy, he's little too", Grandpa asks him in a gentle voice. "Look, when you were his age, we all looked after you so you wouldn't fall over, we played and did all your chores. Why are you teasing him now? You think he likes it when you do that to him?"

"Yes, he does!" Erik shouted, laughing. Mother shrugged her shoulders in disbelief. Even she, who knows them best in this world, couldn't figure out if Erik really believed what he was saying or didn't understand what Grandpa had asked him. After all, who knows what's in the mind of such a small child! Because although he is the big brother and looks huge when the kids are next to each other, he is not far from being still... small.

"We see him that big and have too high expectations of him, I think. We want him to be responsible and pick up his toys, put his clothes back on when he undresses, play nicely, apologize when he makes a mistake and so on", says the father. "After all, he's still a child. A little one."

"You're right", says mother. "When he's next to Dodo, Erik looks like a giant to me. I see Dodo on the carpet, crawling like a glob of cat, and he's so long in my arms that I struggle to hold him. Oh, unforgiving time! These little souls grow up so fast, and I feel I don't enjoy them enough. I don't have enough time in the day to do everything I want to do. The housework never ends, professional duties also knock at the door, and so little time is actually spent with the children... I resent that we are more concerned with their physical "growth" than their education, their soul. Speaking of education, let me disagree. I'm of the opinion that even though he's very young, now is the time he needs to be taught to put his dirty socks in the laundry basket, pick up his toys after playing, or pick up his own water bottle if he sees it on the table and reaches for it. You don't have to see this as exploitation. On the contrary, you're doing him a favour in the long term, because you're teaching him to become responsible and independent. He doesn't have to depend on you for a drink of water. Let's differentiate between pampering, convenience and responsibility", she concludes as she prepares dinner. Silence has settled over the house. After the evening bath, both boys had fallen asleep, and parents and grandparents could have a well-deserved moment of relief and a break for grown-up talk.

The next day, Erik still hadn't forgotten about the doctor's visit and the prick. So, he came up with the idea of a new game.

"Look, Dodo, I'm the doctor, and you stay and let me take some blood! Don't cry, you're a big boy, and it only hurts a little when you get a prick, okay? Then when I take out the needle, you're fine. I'll give you a flyer, okay?" He taps him lightly on the shoulder, as a sign that they've got things straight, and the little one looks at him confused and goes off.

"Wait, I said. Don't run, it won't hurt! Don't cry, okay?" And he starts pulling him, holding him down, until mother comes between them.

"Come on, let him go if he doesn't want to play, please! Maybe he wants to play something else now. What do you think about grabbing your baby toy and taking his blood? And we'll leave Dodo alone to play peekaboo. Okay?"

"No. No, no, no. He's sick now and I have to take his blood! Let me play the game like I want to..."

"Of course. It's just..., it would be nice to consider your brother's wishes too", says the mother, confused. She wonders how should she react now, so that no one gets upset and the game can continue in peace?

It quickly occurred to her to take a little break from what she was doing and get into the game, because if it all degenerated into a conflict, she would hardly be able to reconcile the two of them on her own, especially since Erik is very whiny when he's tired.

"Look, I'm the nurse and I'm going to help you hold him, okay? But please get the tests done quickly, like they did for you yesterday, you've seen how unpleasant it is to keep you in there too long, right? Then we'll let him do his business. Is that all right with you? I don't think Dodo would mind if I held him for a while for this operation."

"It's perfect!" says the little boy, finally satisfied.

"I'm so glad you agree. Afterwards, when you've finished your work here at the surgery, you might want to take a break too! In that case, I could invite you both to lunch. What do you think? Would you like some chicken soup?"

"Yeah, I'd love some. But no peppers."

"How's that?"

"And no onions... and no..."

"Where did you hear that? Come on, finish harvesting quickly and tell me about it while we wash our hands!"

"Where? To Matthew."

"Oh my God," exclaimed the mother. "But you used to like vegetables. Doesn't he like them too?"

"No, he doesn't. And he doesn't eat them. He just wants bread with gravy, that's all."

"And what do the teachers think?"

Erik shrugs.

"If Matthew told you to eat chilli peppers tomorrow, would you eat them? Or if he told you to stop eating biscuits, would you?"

"No."

"Well, then why do you listen to this guy? Look, I believe that every human being has to look at everything through his own mind and heart. If someone tells you something, first of all you have to think whether it's true or false. Then you think about what someone else thinks about it, for example someone you trust: your mother, your father, your grandfather, your teacher. Then you also think about what your heart is telling you, what it really wants! Only then do you draw a conclusion! Remember that it's very serious to do something in life just because someone tells you to. You have to do your own research, to see if it's right or wrong, if your action could upset someone or break a rule, to evaluate the consequences of your actions, if you assume those consequences, and only then decide what to do.

Do you understand?"

"Yeah."

"Never mind, we'll talk about it later. You're a good kid and you'll understand. I'm not saying that Matthew is wrong not to eat peppers. Maybe he just doesn't like them. I'm just saying you don't have to do something just because he does. Everyone has his own personality, his own tastes and has a mind to think for himself. Come on, eat it before it gets really cold!"

"But I want you to give it to me!"

Mom turns to him and encourages him:

"Don't you want to eat by yourself, like at the nursery? The ladies tell me you can and you're doing very well. I even watched you at home when you ate rice with milk. You were so hungry that you ate by yourself, and correctly, leaning a little over the table so it wouldn't spill on you, and I saw that you could hold a spoon very well. Congratulations!"

"Yes, but now I want you to help me. Come on, you give it to me."

"It's harder for me to feed you both at once, but if that's what you want, I'll do it. I've noticed you've been imitating Dodo in everything he does. But you know, when you were a little boy, just like him, I did exactly the same things to you. We even held you more than we did with him and played with you more, because at that time you were the only child in the house and had all our attention. We have deprived him of many things, unfortunately," said the mother with regret for her second born, taking a long pause...

"Yes, but I want you to still feed me!" Erik continued.

Mother resigned herself silently. She knew there was no point in continuing. For some time now, Erik is having a fantastic regression. She'd read about it in several places and had been glad for a long time that things were going well, but it seemed to have started later in his life, only when the baby began to wander around the house and rummage through the toys, and when he began to be fed at the table like everyone else. He initially fought back at the toys, arguing that many were his and he didn't want to share them. Then, he made a scene of all beauty when he found it in his table chair. He has a very good sense of propriety, and there was no way to leave the baby there. Luckily Santa took pity on the little guy and brought him a chair, which Erik obviously tested many times. But things took a turn for the worse when he started imitating the baby, also spelling out "ma-ma-ma", asking to be fed again by his parents, to sleep in his crib or to receive milk several times a day in a baby bottle. He didn't get it every time, obviously, and from here uncountable riots.

"Mommy, you don't have to get milk every time Dodo is breastfed. He's still very small and that's why he needs milk. But your body needs something else. You need to eat fruit, vegetables, meat, nuts..."

"But I also want some... Because I like it too. Pleeease!

4. DIAGNOSIS HITS PARENTS LIKE LIGHTNING

The negotiations continued for a long time and the parents often responded to the child's insistence. He's only a little boy. And besides, milk isn't the real issue they need to focus on at the moment.

It was April 1st when the mother had a call from the doctor. She seemed suspicious that she had called her herself, as she had only kept in touch with her resident until then.

"I understand that you have the results and that it's something very serious, if you called me yourself, and I suppose it's not April Fool's", the mother tried to keep a half optimistic tone.

"Unfortunately, it is. The test results have come and I don't have very good news. But it's not very serious either, don't panic! I just did what you asked me to do, to investigate in detail. Isn't that what you wanted?"

"Yes" said the mother, on one side shocked and upset by the news, on the other happy that at least she would find out what was wrong with the big boy and they could solve the problem once and for all. "Tell me: is it the milk or the gluten? I've had milk tested before and it wasn't very relevant then."

"Unfortunately, gluten is the problem. But please come to the Institute tomorrow to talk more! I'll explain everything to you! If you can come alone, without the child, that would be even better!"

"How was the meeting?" asks the father the next day. "I called you a few times. Is the boy okay?"

"Yes. But he has to go on a strict gluten-free diet forever. And lactose free for three months at first."

The Father takes a long break on the phone:

"Is it that bad? Really that strict?"

"Yes. But the doctor kept insisting, saying it's good he doesn't have anything else, that if he had diabetes, he'd be addicted to insulin... and that the only treatment was food. Anyway... I really don't know what to say. The shock is too much now. It's one thing to diet for three months, it's another to diet for life. But... we'll manage somehow."

"Yeah" the father concludes. "Is he okay otherwise? By the sound of your voice, you sound scared. Anything else you want to tell me?"

"No. It's just... the doctor insisted we read all the labels very carefully. Her recommendation was to get a magnifying glass to carry in our bag, because some labels have very small writing. And to read absolutely everything. Even on fever syrups. Many contain gluten, it seems. Or there are certain excipients that hide gluten. We need to do some serious research, know the list and know how to avoid them. Basically, the doctor recommended that we should have the greatest confidence in consuming food products that have the cut wheat spike symbol (Crossed Grain logo accompanied by the licence number), the most stringent food standard obtained through a monitored external audit process. They are certified as 100% safe. In the case of the others, which say gluten-free only (in English or any foreign language), the manufacturer declares under his own responsibility that they are gluten-free, following internal control tests for the presence of gluten. Celiacs should avoid eating processed foods that do not have any indication of gluten presence or absence on the label. This means that, first of all, we must reflexively read all labels. Because gluten can hide where you don't even think about it. Did you know that it can even be in the banal, frozen fries that many restaurants roast? Well, that's just one example. That's why I'm a little concerned. I guess it's not all as simple as it seems at first sight. But... taking things one step at a time, we'll see where we end up."

In mother's heart a war had already begun. She felt powerless, wronged, punished. She didn't even realize how she'd made her way home. In her mind were playing all sorts of images of Erik playing happy with flour. He was a dough lover. Among his favorite activities with his mother was baking. They would make doughnuts, pancakes, apple pancakes and pizza together. Their work would turn the kitchen into a battlefield, and the child and his mother were often covered from head to toe in flour.

Such a sad thing that they would never have any more of it. The mother's image of his tender hands trying to shape a piece of crust runs through her mind. Then he sinks his clenched fists into the stretched hull to break off another piece. He spills a glass of water over his allotted flour while his mother's back is turned and laughs ear to ear as his little basin falls to the tiles and he runs his hands through his hair in a gesture of: 'oh my, what a terrible thing I've done!' The father opens the kitchen door and scolds him, smiling, 'What are you two doing here? And you're both going in the shower, right?' he says, amused, after greeting them and giving them a quick kiss, trying to get out as quickly as possible so he doesn't get his work clothes dirty... the thread breaks. Mother's eyes glaze over. Tears roll down her cheeks, uncontrollably. 'It's not that serious!' she hears the doctor's voice again in her mind. 'He can keep to her diet and he'll be fine.' Yes, he'll be fine for sure, she tries to cheer herself up. We'll find other equally exciting pursuits, she tells herself.

But the battle in her soul continues in the days and months ahead. Because the child regime is a team effort, and she suddenly finds herself in the position of trainer for minds of all ages and cultures.

She's no stranger to the gluten-free diet, having been on one herself for several months, a few years ago when she was gluten-free. But then she knew in principle not to eat bread and other flours, and she was happy to eat a salad or fish and chips in a restaurant or when visiting friends. Now, however, things have become very complicated. The child's dietary restrictions are very strict and his social life seems to suffer greatly, with the harsh diet affecting everyone's emotional state.

5. RESEARCH ON CELIAC DISEASE AND THE STRICT GLUTEN-FREE DIET

What is the first thing any patient does before or after talking to the doctor? Do further research. Well, since after the 2-hour discussion with the pediatrician, the mother still felt foggy, she took a look on the internet, hoping it would clear up and find some lifesaving solutions. For starters, she discovered that there was a celiac website and social media pages dedicated to celiacs in their area. There, however, discussions are divided between those who are just starting out or being diagnosed and those who have had the disease for a few years and are very susceptible to contamination. Contamination that is talked about at every turn in the celiac world, unfortunately. At the moment, the parents don't know how serious Erik's situation is, but they decide that as long as it's up to them, they'll do the best they can. So, they decide to eat only certified gluten-free products and to give up anything commercially processed or frozen. In other words, to eat as fresh, natural and balanced as possible.

"Good. But then what is the child allowed to eat?" asks Grandpa one day, puzzled and sad.

"Anything but gluten", said the father, trying not to scare him too much.

"So, no bread. He needs a special bread, bought or made for him. And we can't make him anything with country flour... Is meat allowed?"

"Yes. If it's unprocessed, unwashed or commercially

prepared meat. Backyard poultry is fine. But don't spike the soup with borscht."

"That's right", Grandma completes. "Borscht is made from bran, which comes from wheat, and contains gluten, along with barley and rye. That's what you said, right?"

"That's right. And no noodles, no spices. We can use gluten-free noodles, they're available on the market from rice or even corn, or substitute rice, or just put more vegetables. And tomatoes for the soup... either fresh, or just homemade preserved, sterilized with no preservatives. Regular ones may contain gluten."

"Lots of restrictions", Grandpa concludes.

"Indeed! But unfortunately, there's nothing we can do about it. We adapt as we go. We will see, however, how we'll proceed with the kindergarten. The children there are given a fixed menu and we need to have a serious discussion with the school management about this health problem and see what solutions we can find. In the meantime, we are doing some more research to see what else we need to take into account for the boy to be well."

"Mommy, am I not allowed to eat bread any more?" asks Erik, who must have been eavesdropping on the adults' discussion.

"No, dear. But from now on you're only allowed to eat a special bread."

"Why am I only allowed to eat one particular bread, Mommy?"

"Because the doctor said so, after the tests."

"And why did she say that, Mommy?"

"So, your tummy won't hurt anymore, baby. Apparently, the reason your tummy hurts is because of the gluten containing flour. That's it. From now on, if we watch what we eat and stick to this strict diet, you'll feel much better."

"But why, Mommy? Why did my tummy hurt?"

"Because your tummy is special, it doesn't accept gluten. And then we'll do everything we can to make it better. I promise. But don't be sad. This bread is good too, you can still eat bread with butter or honey in the morning."

"Hooray, cries the child, happy. I want honey with bread now, Mommy!"

"It's not morning now. It's lunchtime. And at noon we eat cooked food. Do you want soup or main course?" asked Mommy. She knows this tactic usually works, to let him choose from the two types of food provided. He's tired anyway and wouldn't have eaten both, so she's happy if she can get him to try something.

"But then can I have some bread and honey, please!"

"Okay, fine. Only after you eat as little as possible, that will be your dessert."

After lunch, when everyone settles down to their midday nap, Mother continues her research into the illness. That's how she discovers that there are several situations in which people can keep this kind of diet. So, there is gluten sensitivity/intolerance, wheat/gluten allergy and celiac disease, all of which have gluten-free diet recommendations. When they hear about gluten, many people think of intolerance or allergy. Few know about celiac disease. In the case of celiac disease, the diet is much stricter, that's where the contamination story comes in and the diet is unfortunately lifelong, as it is an autoimmune disease. But people think they know it all and come up with all sorts of stories like: well, I know someone who had it and got better. Or: my child too went on a diet for a few months and then that was it, no more. You'll see it works out. These are the most unpleasant things a celiac patient can hear. In fact, I don't even know what's worse. To be pitied? Or encouraged that everything will be fine, when there is currently no cure for it? Mother thinks about both aspects and doesn't know what to think. Of course, it's our duty to believe in science, that some groundbreaking treatment will be discovered by the time he grows up, and to believe first of all in God, that He knows best how to put things right. But the reality is that right now, strictly at this moment, we need to focus on a strict regime. And it is not easy. And we need it more in that sense than in the sense of lengthen my days, Lord, let the strawberries ripen, as the folks say!

So, the next step is to join as many celiac groups as possible to keep up to date with what's new in the field. Getting familiar with the restrictions and the new lifestyle that will become the whole family's, looking for recipes for bread, seeing with what we can replace many of the dishes they used to like, how to make a delicious cake, how to proceed with food when we go somewhere and so on.

6. REPLACING GLUTEN PRODUCTS IN THE HOME AND FAMILY MEALS

"How are we going to proceed with the meals from now on?" asked the father puzzled. "I think we should all eat the same, to make it easier for us and not to contaminate him."

"Agree", said mother. "I suggest we don't buy wheat bread in the house at all. What does that mean? First of all, replacing this staple with gluten-free. This automatically means an increase in the daily cost of bread, as gluten-free bread is 4-5 times more expensive than regular bread. Beyond the increased price, it's about changing lifestyle and denying the body an element at the bottom of the food pyramid. For us, I don't see a big problem. On the contrary, it also seemed to me that we were eating too many bakery products. But what do we do with the baby? The doctor said not to deprive him of gluten, until at least a year and a half, when he could be tested. So, what should we do with him?"

"Well, we feed him gluten occasionally", Dad said.

"Okay. But I can't buy a loaf of bread to give him a slice. Since we've agreed that we're not going to eat gluten in the house."

"Of course not! But we will give him small, manageable, controllable things like apple with cookies, grits, or cereal with milk, anything that can be prepared in a separate bowl to spoon out without crumbs around the house that could contaminate Erik. The rest, such as breadsticks, puffs, bagels, bread, he will mostly eat outside the house, either when you go out or in the grandparents' yard, and preferably when Erik is not around, to avoid getting his hands on it."

"That's a really good idea! This way we don't deprive our little one of gluten and products that are necessary for his harmonious growth, and we don't contaminate Erik either. The truth is that with such young children, the problem of contamination is very difficult. You can't really control them from touching each other, putting their fingers in each other's mouths, putting their mouths on each other's baby bottles or water bottles, offering each other tea from the same cup, and so on."

"You're right! And by the way, I've noticed that Erik is very generous with food, despite the fact that he doesn't want to share toys under any circumstances. So generous that sometimes I don't know how to react anymore. For example, if he gets a grape or a piece of apple in his hand, he comes and puts it in Dodo's mouth too. In turn, the little one puts his fingers in his mouth, checking if he has something to eat or if he is ready to play. It would be funny what's going on, if it wasn't so serious in terms of contamination", sigh the parents.

"It is! But some things we can control, some things we can't. It's beyond our power. God willing, we'll see what happens."

"What about the dishes in which we serve Dodo gluten-free food?"

"We'll try to use the same dishes as much as possible: bowl, kettle, spoon, cup, which we'll label and put on a separate shelf. But we have to be very careful with the water bottles, which they have started sharing."

"Erik!" cried Dad. Come here and let me tell you something! "Did you know that every child has to drink from his own water bottle?"

"Yes", said the little boy. "Mother keeps telling me this."

"But do you know why?" The little boy shrugs his shoulders and the father continues: "Look, every person must have his own glass or cup, because that way bacteria and viruses can't spread from one to another. In your case, it's even more than that, you're not allowed to drink from someone else's container because you can contaminate yourself. Meaning you'll put your mouth where someone with gluten has already put it, and you'll accidentally pick up gluten, and you're likely to get a tummy ache afterwards. So, do you understand why do you have to take care of your bottle every time, wherever you are? The same thing we need to teach Dodo when he grows up, because this can also keep us from many other diseases. Will you help me do that, please? If you repeat it over and over again, he'll understand better from you!"

"Sure, Daddy!" He then picked up his water bottle and walked over to Dodo, pretending to tell him: "Look, this is your bottle. You're not allowed to put your mouth on mine, it's not hygienic for me to drink from yours either. Come on, drink from yours if you want. Can I help you?" Erik asked, as his father looked at them from a distance, satisfied and at peace.

"Mommy, Dodo has sprinkled biscuits on his face", Erik shouted at the top of his lungs, as the little boy pulled out a gluten biscuit from nowhere.

"Oh, God, where have you been hiding it, child?" asked Mom, remembering that a biscuit had fallen out of his hand outside, and as there was no rubbish bin around, she had put it in the pram bin to throw it at home. And the baby now looked in there for toys and found it. "It's no problem, sweetie", she then tried to reassure Erik. "Look, he didn't mean to, he's little too. Let me wash your face and everything will be fine. You'll see! He's little too, what can we do? As he grows up, we'll keep talking to him about your gluten intolerance and he'll have to respect your lifestyle, maybe even adopt it in your presence. For now, we do what we think is best for both of you, but there is no way to force or condition him to do anything specific. We want you both to be happy", explained Erik's mother.

7. WHAT IS GLUTEN AND WHAT IS THE DIFFERENCE BETWEEN INTOLERANCE, ALLERGY AND CELIAC DISEASE

The news of the child's illness spread quickly among family and acquaintances. The mother then found out, no surprise at all, that many people have no idea what gluten is, the ingredients it is found in or how it can affect the bodies of celiac patients. In this situation, the mother decided to do some thorough research and even write down some facts to give to her loved ones. This way, she will bring them up to speed while saving time and energy.

"Gluten is a protein found in wheat, barley and rye. It's the "glue" in flour, metaphorically speaking. I found this explanation somewhere and loved it. Well, automatically you should avoid products containing: wheat, barley or rye. The point is, patients and their families need to educate themselves a bit from a nutritional, food point of view. They need to know what certain foods are made from. Because borscht, for example, is made from bran, which comes from wheat. The bulgur or arrowroot from which they make porridge is also derived from wheat. Flour can also be found in tomato sauce, frozen potato chips, mustard, grated cornflour or even in cans. So, danger is everywhere and all labels must be read carefully. There is no way you can stick to this strict diet without reading up on these things, without having access to the minimum information on ingredients and recipes.

Then there is the problem of contamination. Even if they are gluten-free at their core, some grains, such as oats or corn, can be highly contaminated if they have been planted near wheat, barley, rye, or if they have been milled or processed in the same factories as gluten-containing grains. So, in this case they too will be excluded from the celiacs' diet, and celiacs will only be allowed to eat products marked with the symbol of the cut off grain", explains the mother. She has said this poem so many times that she has learnt it by heart and found herself talking casually about gluten as if she has been doing this for a long time.

But the contamination doesn't end there. It's a sensitive subject, something about which they find out something every day, which requires a lot of attention and the awareness and cooperation of everyone around them. Because celiacs are extremely easy to contaminate.

But coming back to the 3: allergy, intolerance and celiac disease, here are some essential facts about each one, in a way that everyone can understand, explained by Dr. Lidia Cremer, PhD, Research Scientist, Trainer, Nutrition Consultant and... patient:

Celiac Disease:
Autoimmune condition that can start at any age. It affects about 1% of the population and usually occurs in genetically predisposed individuals when it could be triggered by some environmental factors. In these individuals, after ingestion of gluten-containing foods, the immune system begins to react abnormally and generates a series of antibodies that attacks the lining of the small intestine itself, leading to a marked inflammatory process in the small intestine, with destruction of the intestinal villi, which are responsible for absorbing nutrients from food. This is also the reason why many patients suffer from iron deficiency anaemia, as Erik did. Other common nutritional deficiencies in patients with Celiac Disease, besides iron, can be: Calcium, Magnesium, Zinc, vitamins: B12, folic acid, D, E, K.

Symptoms are very varied in celiac disease (more than 300 symptoms and associated conditions are reported) and consist of digestive and/or extradigestive disorders, and the only currently accepted treatment is a strict gluten-free diet for life. Unfortunately, the diet does not cure the disease, but it can keep it under control so that the patient can have a normal life.

Nowadays, diagnosis is made according to internationally agreed protocols. For children, depending on age, following blood tests (usually without the need for endoscopy with biopsy). Here there are two situations: children under 2 years do: Total IgA, anti-transglutaminase Ac (IgA, IgG), anti-gliadin deamidated Ac (IgA, Ig); and those over 2 years of age: Total IgA, Ac anti-transglutaminase (IgA, IgG), Ac anti-endomysium (IgA, IgG). For adults, blood tests are recommended first: total IgA, anti-transglutaminase (IgA, IgG), anti-endomysium (IgA, IgG). The presence of specific Ac will then be correlated with upper gastrointestinal endoscopy with biopsies.

Wheat allergy:
Wheat allergy is an immune system reaction whereby the body produces specific antibodies to wheat proteins. People with wheat allergy have developed specific IgE antibodies to wheat and so their body rejects products containing it. In the case of allergy, the reaction is immediate, in contrast to intolerance, where it can take several days for symptoms to appear.

Non-celiac gluten sensitivity/intolerance:
This condition is up to 10 times more common than celiac disease. It is induced by ingestion of gluten and manifests itself by intestinal and/or extra-intestinal symptoms that subside and may eventually disappear over time after the removal of gluten from the diet. As there are no specific markers for this condition, the diagnosis is made only after excluding celiac disease and wheat allergy and instituting a gluten-free diet, if the body responds positively.

8. BEWARE OF CARELESSNESS. INSPIRATIONAL STORIES AND LIFE-SAVING IDEAS

People with food allergies or intolerances experience all sorts of challenges. They have to be constantly aware of their diet, read product labels, ask the waiter about the ingredients, "if they dare to eat out", and be aware of nutritional deficiencies that may arise due to dietary restrictions.

This can become frustrating both for them, and for parents or other relatives, as they not only have to be mindful of what they offer to their child, but also of those around them, who are often so generous as to offer gluten products to others, even when they know about the problem they have.

One day, Erik and his best friend were riding their bikes around the block. It was a typical summer day, and the kids were thirsty. Just as the parents are rummaging in their backpacks for water, they hear the buddy's voice:

"I want biscuits!"

His father complies. He takes the bottle of water, then takes out the food, and after offering the little boy his favourite biscuits, he reaches out his hand to Erik and says to his father:

"I'll give it to him, all right? They're organic!"

"No. No" cried Mom and Dad in one voice. "They have gluten!"

The other child's parent took a step back and said in a lost voice:

"That's right. They do! Sorry. I didn't realise."

Erik's father continued to argue with Erik, telling him about gluten-containing products, but the upset mother was still in shock. She was also looking for gluten-free biscuits in her bag, and her hands were visibly shaking. All sorts of scenarios ran through her mind. Then she felt vulnerable again. She felt a terrible feeling of isolation from the diagnosis. It was too much strain and she wanted to cry.

"How can I control what happens at the kindergarten? Or at after school or wherever he goes later! If even people close to us, with whom we spend time every day, forget such important things, what expectations and demands should I have of others? I can only pray to God that it will be okay, no matter what! After all, all these autoimmune diseases, hard to understand, I think only in Him to give us hope. We are at His mercy. Lord, give us the strength to carry on, to do everything that is in our power, and further on You will take care of us, so Your will be done", said the mother in thought, as she offered the little boy the biscuits.

"You don't have to feel bad for your gesture", she added, addressing the neighbour! "Very few people know the facts about celiac disease and the strict gluten-free diet. It would be useful to educate schools about allergies and food intolerances. There are many people who are allergic to egg or cow's milk protein, for example. That way, if people learn about these things at school, later on there would be educated staff in the HoReCa industry, where there is a great need for people who know about contamination, its effects or first aid gestures in case of serious allergic reactions."

"Yes. That wouldn't be bad at all. Personally, until you told me about Erik's problem, I had no idea that such thing existed, and especially that it could be so serious. It's sad that this happens to people, especially children. I don't know what I would do if my child was in this situation. Honestly. I compassionate you", said the neighbor's father.

"Yeah. It's sad. But there's nothing we can do, unfortunately. Just hope for a miracle and look for the best solutions to be better off in the present. As for the future, we'll see what it holds."

"Yes. It's important to be positive", said father, who was still hoping that a cure would come sooner.

"I know what you're thinking" smiled Mom, sympathetically. "But I still think it could be many years before a cure is found. And I need things for my child now. Now, you understand?"

"What are you talking about?" Erik said. "Understand what?"

"Baby, I told you there are other kids in this world who eat gluten-free. Just like there are others who eat without cow's milk protein, without eggs, or who have an even more strict diet because they are allergic to histamine. Would you like to meet them, talk to them about their diet, how they feel, play together and eat the same way?"

"Yes. Sure. And shall we take my friend Ana? And

Matthew?"

"Why not? You can take her as well, and Matthew. I'm sure they'll like gluten-free food too. Gluten-free bread is delicious too."

"What are you up to?" Dad asked.

"Since we have the problem, and I see him so frustrated when others eat something else around, all I can think about is making him feel better. It would be ideal if there was a nursery for kids like that. But it's hard with the distance, the schedule, the age... being that many are perhaps of different ages, from different areas or even far away if they are in the same town. So, I had an idea: what if we made a club for children with intolerances? Or something like that? Where children could meet occasionally (like weekends), and do different activities. Like making music, or doing crafts, or doing homework? That way, they could make friends with children of similar ages, spend time together, eat meals together, develop a sense of belonging and perhaps regain their self-confidence. They could also learn about their diet, how to feed themselves so they don't have nutritional deficiencies, and they could take part in nutrition lessons and maybe even cooking workshops."

"Yes. I want to bake cookies", said the child, who eavesdropped on the adults' excited conversation. "Shall we make some gluten-free sweets? And lactose-free?"

"Sure. We'll do it at home tonight!" said Mom, without repeating all the above explanations. Then she goes on to tell the two adults about other fantastic projects in her ideal gluten-free world. "One thing that really worries me is the lack of gluten-free restaurants. Why would I lie that I'm not frustrated about this, when I am? We're trying to come to terms with the fact that there's NOTHING left to go out for, but we actually used to go out a lot and I find it sad that we can't do that anymore. At exactly 7 days old, we took Erik out to a quiet terrace between the blocks", she remembers. "We did this before we had kids and even with them small. Now, it's hard enough to isolate ourselves or limit ourselves to plain lemon water at restaurants. And let's just say we do it, because we have no choice. What will his life be like? What will he do when he's older and his mates invite him for a juice or a cake? He will be excluded from many circles for this reason. In our town, for example, there are very few, if any, restaurants. Gluten-free, I mean."

"You're right. But what can we do?"

"It would be nice to have a gluten-free place. I've given this idea a lot of thought, but ultimately, I don't know how much it would help. More helpful would be to have gluten-free food, safely prepared, in almost every restaurant. That would make things a lot easier. And I also have an idea of how that could be done. But it takes a lot of money, and I haven't found a sponsor yet."

"Amaze us!" said the father, and the two men listened with interest to the idea of a life-saving business for celiacs and possibly other people with food allergies and intolerances.

"Firstly, there could be an online platform to run the programme. For the sake of exercise, let's call it 'Gluten-Free friends at the table'. Interested restaurants, whether stand-alone or in hotels and so on, would sign up to the platform. They will display their affiliation, their 'Gluten-Free Friends at the Table' status, both on their website and prominently at the entrance, so that people know they have gluten-free, non-contaminated food. Because that's the fear of all celiacs, that food in restaurants is contaminated in the kitchen, where there's a lot of buzz and no cooking on separate lines.

"Well, how can it not be contaminated? You imagine they wouldn't be willing to create separate lines to cook the food. Maybe they have one customer a week with such problems, it is not profitable to do that, logistically speaking."

"Agree! But what if all those restaurants signed up to the 'Gluten-Free Friends at the Table' platform contracted with a catering company that would be exclusively gluten-free, possibly even lactose-free, and would deliver such products to them on request. You'll say: yes, but until they cook, until they deliver... Well, do you think it's better for these people not to go out at all? Do you have any idea how many celiacs I've met lately who don't go out at all? Or if they do, they waste a lot of time cooking at home beforehand, so they can eat out with the others, out of their sufferers... A celiac has a different schedule anyway. He will enjoy this outing like you can't imagine. And generally, people with such problems schedule their appointments in advance, so they could call the restaurant and say that tomorrow for their reservation at 18.00, they would like to order a portion of gluten-free pasta, a dessert etc. Or they could call the canteen directly and say where and at what time to place their order. Ideally, this could also be done that day, 2-3 hours before the outing, if something from the daily menu is ordered. Restaurants can have a separate menu on their website and people will order from there. And so that there are no problems with delivery, the food could be eaten straight from the containers it is brought in. Like Chinese food, for example. But at least the man doesn't have to worry about cooking beforehand. And this service can be extended to events, weddings, christenings, cocktail parties... there are many who go hungry at such gatherings because they don't dare to go with the sandwich from home, or who take the risk and get contaminated, then lie there for days until they recover."

"It's nice what you say there. But it sounds like fantasy to me. It's hard with transportation in the first place. If they're going to have multiple orders at the same time, in very remote locations, what are they going to do? Plus, ideally, they'd also deliver hot food. Plus, you have to have people specifically for that, who only carry gluten-free food."

"True. But not impossible, in my opinion! I just need to find the person who sees the potential in the whole thing."

"Yeah. It's a very good idea, and one that would solve the dining out problem very well. It remains to be seen what the restaurants think now!"

"I don't see why they wouldn't agree. As long as you bring them customers, basically. I mean, would you rather lose a group of 5-7 people because one delivery eats at your table? Because the same group can be accepted by the restaurant across the street under the conditions mentioned. In addition, the catering company could also give a token commission to the restaurant.

Or think of a formula in which the restaurant could earn something extra. But let's just think of the publicity they can get on Tripadvisor, for example."

"Yes. It's a niche that can be exploited very well from a business point of view. It's a pity we're emotionally involved in this", Dad said.

9. THE NEIGHBOUR AND SNACKING

Leaving out all the gluten products in the house and replacing them with gluten-free options has brought everyone a sense of contentment, of peace, of relief. Mom had gathered several large bags of flour, cornmeal, pasta and spaghetti, grits, breakfast cereal, lasagna sheets, yeast, spices, and lots of sweets, which the little boy received from everyone who came to visit, but he understood that he didn't have to unwrap and consume them all at once, so Mom put them away properly each time. And now they collected them and had them donated. All of them.

Replacing the products with gluten-free ones turned out to be not as hard as it is expensive. Fortunately, all kinds of gluten-free products are now available, from various types of flour to spaghetti, pasta, "grits" - a kind of ground, shredded rice. These would be the basics, but then, on closer inspection, products that are gluten-free but likely to be contaminated, such as cornflour, sauces, ketchup, even mustard, spices and more, need to be replaced. Absolutely all ingredients should be read with the utmost care.

"How are you handling the new lifestyle?" asks a neighbour one day.

"It's not as hard as it sounds. I mean, at least it's not impossible. We're lucky that we're near the big supermarket chains, which are stocked with such products."

"Yeah, but I guess they're pretty expensive..."

"Well, yes. That's quite an important point. You're right, a small bread, not as big as a regular baguette, costs 5-6 times as much. Depends on where you buy it and on what days. But we have no choice. The important thing is that the boy gets well. These aspects are less important to us now."

"Of course. I didn't mean it that way. I imagine that is the most important thing. I was just saying that the financial aspect is not to be underestimated."

"That's true. But one thing that I find even harder is that products are not found everywhere. Unfortunately, even bread is not always available in the big chain stores. We had the rather unpleasant surprise of not finding bread when we went shopping."

"And how do you act in this case?"

"We usually stock up with more than one pack when we find it, so we don't get surprised. If, however, it does happen, we always have gluten-free flour in the house. Recently we've also bought a bread machine, because we'd like to make bread exclusively at home in the future. It's pretty easy to make and comes out fluffy, tasty, it's wonderful. We all eat it, with pleasure, reliving the times when we used to heat up the bread oven almost daily with all sorts of goodies. I've tried several bread recipes, but they didn't turn out so well, so this machine is making all its money. Instead, I've become an expert on gluten-free muffins and pies. They never used to be as good as they are now. They're wonderful."

"I'd like to give my daughter something to snack on. How are we proceeding with Erik?"

"You can give her that without any problems. We have some snacks in our backpack. I used to always put crackers, breadsticks, or other snacks in my bag, because you never know when a kid comes along and eats something outside and obviously, he wants some. We often gather here between the blocks in the evenings with several moms to let the kids play. All fine and nice until one of them brings out the cookie case or the bag of breadsticks. Then my Erik is left open-mouthed at the child who hands the bag to everyone in turn. I watch him closely and notice that as he approaches, he takes a step back and stares at me. I always try to be on my toes when these things happen.

And unfortunately, they are daily and unavoidable. Parents, out of a desire to feed their children something, anything, would rather feed them while they play than not eat at all. I understand very well, because we have been in this situation ourselves. But for us it is even harder because often the products are not similar and we cannot have diversity. I remember one day when a child got hungry and shouted to his mother on the balcony to come down and get him, what do you think? Pizza. You can imagine what was in my mind and heart then. I had breadsticks and crackers. It's not all the same. Where am I gonna get pizza? I haven't even experimented with making super pizza flatbreads at home yet. Besides, it takes time. So, there are situations where I just don't have similar products to offer him and he stays back and stares longingly at the kids. In their mouths, to be specific. I pull him aside many times and tell him: 'I know you wanted to. You wish, don't you?' He nods affirmatively. Then I say, 'I'm sorry you can't. What are we suppose to do if your tummy doesn't accept gluten? We have to love her just the way she is and be glad we can offer her other things to her satisfaction.' I don't know whether or not I'm doing it right, but for now that's all I can do. I'm frustrated? Yes. Very. I've been thinking about seeing a therapist. And take him to it. To make it easier for him to accept the situation and not feel excluded, isolated, strange... but do you know what the psychologist's response was? A special acquaintance of mine, whom I met many years ago through my professional work, with whom I later had a brief but beautiful collaboration, and with whom I resonated because we were somehow facing the same problem in our personal lives: children were long overdue in both of our lives. So, I have a lot of confidence in this person, especially since she actually works with children with various issues. Well, her answer was as logical as it can be, and it sounded like this: 'Do you think that if you bring your child to me for therapy I start talking to him directly about gluten, about what he is allowed to eat and what not? Obviously not. It's an extremely sensitive subject and you hardly get to it. I can coach him in different games and we can migrate in that direction, but the subject is sensitive. And... on the other hand, do you think he'll trust me, whom I'm basically a stranger to him, more than you, who are the being closest to his soul that he trusts the most in this world? My dear, you are the one who must speak most openly to your child. Explain to him in his own understanding, but speak to him as frankly as you would it, if you were in front of an adult. Even if he's little, he understands very well, believe me! Take every opportunity to explain, encourage him to ask you if he has any questions, and to tell you about his feelings. If you have any queries or get stuck at any point, you can always ask again and I will guide you. But trust me. No one in this world can explain to him better than family why he's not allowed to eat one way or the other. If you ask several psychologists, they're all likely to tell you something different. I don't dispute that there are colleagues in the profession who would promise to help you, to work magic, and to go to therapy. But trust me, I know you, I know your story, and I don't want to put you in the position of spending money for nothing. It would be easy for me to take your money, call you in for sessions, but that's not the solution. Time will solve everything. It will get into your reflex to eat this way; you will become so comfortable with the way you eat that in the future these things will just be memories.' God, help it happen! I try to talk to him as much as I can. I know it is very important that he understands exactly how things are, that his mind stops questioning all the time, that he accepts the situation as it is, and that his subconscious stops working against him. And us, all of us. The mental setting is extremely important. We need to be at peace with the fact that everything happens for a purpose in life, to take only the good side of things, to try to find only what is beautiful in everything around us. Let's be optimistic and confident! Let's be glad that we have detected the cause of tummy aches, and that already after a short time of starting the regime we can see changes for the better, let's thank God for enlightening our steps to find the truth and the way now, while he is still small, before he develops other related conditions. Because lack of diet can lead to many other conditions. So, it seems we are lucky that God has worked in our favor and we were able to learn about this problem early enough.”

"Yes. Maybe you're right”, my neighbor says. “However, unlike simple gluten intolerance, which I've heard can pass in a few years, celiac disease is rarer. Do you have any idea how many people have it?”

"I don't have a clear picture yet. I am just researching national and global statistics. I had read that it is about 1% of the population, but the condition is greatly under-diagnosed (up to 83% of celiac disease cases are thought to be undiagnosed or misdiagnosed). Here's our case: we've been to so many doctors..., if we hadn't gotten to this dedicated doctor who loves children and had the inspiration to do the necessary tests... I think it would have been a long time before we found out.”

"Did you know you can get financial aid from the state? I heard from someone who has this problem and also gets other benefits.”

"According to the law, in our country children with celiac disease can get an income from the state if they are classified as disabled. This can be obtained at the request of the family and is only valid for children, not adults. I personally, and I assume what I say, although many may condemn me for this, have decided with my husband not to get the child a disability certificate.”

"Why? It's important to get a little help from the State.”

"Possibly. But the long-term psychological impact seems more serious to me", says Mom. “I remember when I was little and used to wear glasses. I wore glasses all my childhood. And many times, I endured the mockery of my classmates, who shouted at me: four-eyed stove! Kids make all sorts of bad jokes. They use the term 'handicapped' in a pejorative sense and without the person having a real health problem, but when they do, you figure it out. I'm not saying celiac isn't a serious problem. On the contrary. Even the boy's doctor pointed this out to us at the first check-up we went for: ‘Don't look at him as being good-looking on the outside, cheerful and energetic. He is a very sick child. Very sick on the inside, believe me!’ Her words have echoed in my mind for a long time, and they surface like oil in my mind every time someone asks me: but what if he gets contaminated, or if he gets a little taste, too, on a whim? But now is not the time to go back to the issue of contamination or lack of education. The bottom line is that we are willing to make a financial sacrifice for the sake of his psychological comfort."

"Indeed, if you look at it that way"", said the neighbour, "you may be right. After all, Erik is a perfectly normal child. He's no different from any of ours. They play together very nicely, they argue and reconcile, he's smart, kind and sensitive. I only know he has a problem because we know each other well and you told me about it. Otherwise, I would have thought he was just another child. I would never have suspected that he lives a gluten-free life. He's just as energetic as everyone else and can do absolutely the same things, no matter what."

"Exactly! This is a great relief to us. I'll leave you now, I have to go shopping with the boys. Their father has a little more work to do after work and we need to stock up on the necessities, which you can't get at the stores between the blocks. Then we have to prepare dinner, hang out the laundry left in the washing machine and get the clothes ready for tomorrow's nursery. Come on, Erik, are you ready to go?"

"No. We'll stay a little longer, please!"

"Five more minutes and we're done. We have to go, because we have a lot to do."

"No, we don't. I want to be here. We're not leaving!"

"Honey, I feel sorry for you. I know you were having a great time. I wish I could have left you with the kids to play, but we have to go shopping. Now, while Dodo's still quiet and sitting in the stroller. Here's the deal: do you want to ride the bike or should I put you on the stroller next to him?"

"Yes, yes," he shouts enthusiastically. "Both on the horse. Yeah!"

Mom straightens the stroller, leaving the backrest horizontal. She puts Dodo in the back and Erik in the front and they set off together. It wasn't the first time she'd sat them like this. As she pushes the handle of the cart with one hand and with the other holds Dodo, who has been struggling for a while and trying to get up, Mom thinks how silly they look like this, both perched on the trolley. People look at them on the street and smile. They smile at people in turn and sit there happily perched. Sometimes quietly, sometimes pushing each other, arguing over a toy or shouting until one of them gives in and gets off, most often Dodo, who is carried with difficulty in their arms. This time, however, the journey was in good conditions, so Mom takes advantage of the silence to explain a few more things to Erik:

"Baby, wherever you go from now on, please tell people about celiac disease. They need to understand the implications of the disease, and that their insistence makes you feel uncomfortable, and that on the contrary, it would be very helpful to have their understanding and cooperation. Many people don't know what contamination means and why it is so important, they don't know they can harm you if they insist on offering you gluten products. It's our responsibility and yours to protect you, especially when those around you don't know the problem."

10. THE TASTES BETWEEN SLIDES

Erik asks his mother to go to the park. He's bored of sitting among the blocks alone. And she didn't like it either. Since the pandemic had started, she had memorized all the stones in the neighborhood and had wiped all the curbs clean of dust. She was sorry that she didn't let him socialize like he used to, especially since he was at an age where he should be encouraged to do so. 'What ugly times we live in', she thought. 'We've come to fear each other, to avoid each other...' She helped him cross the street, then let him ride his bike across the narrow sidewalk, narrowed by cars. She quickens her pace too, so as not to let the distance between them grow too much. Dodo speaks cheerfully on his tongue in the cart. He likes that mom is pushing him so fast, almost running. She breathes a sigh of relief, however, when she sees Erik pull up to the curb near the intersection. She keeps explaining not to cross the street alone and she is glad the little boy understands. She helps him cross again and enters the park victorious, shouting:

"To the slides I want!" He sits for a second in place to wait for her and to confirm his agreement, then heads for the playground. Mom's not too happy about it because it's a bit crowded, but a promise is a promise, so she has no choice. She sits with Dodo on a bench, while Erik "parks" his green pedal bike among the children, very proud of it.

A little boy slightly younger than him comes over to inspect the bike. Erik grabs his hand and immediately waves it away:

"No!"

The child resigns and walks away, and Erik looks after the bigger children. He would like to play with them. Under the slides, between the little houses, a guild hides from the burning rays of the sun. Erik enters their midst, wanting to socialize. But he can't get a word in edgeways. He effectively remains stuck, probably waiting for the others to speak.

He would like to approach them somehow, but walks awkwardly in front of them. Finally, he tells them his name and asks them to talk. The children show signs of liking him and agreeing to let him join their gang. The mother watches them from the bench, taking advantage of this quiet moment to feed the baby. When she looks up again, she sees one of the children, who had been rummaging around in his backpack, pull out a bag of sticks and start offering them all. Erik was inside the cottage, and through the small windows the mother no longer had a direct view of him. She wanted to call out to him, to make him pay attention to get out of there, but she felt a lump in her throat and couldn't articulate another word. With her shirt unbuttoned and the baby under her breast, in a split second she was beside them.

"No!" she cries desperately, scaring the children. "Don't give it to him!"

She grabbs the child's hand, while staring at him, checking his hands carefully, lest he had already grabbed something. Erik didn't know how to react. He hadn't done anything wrong. The woman then realized that perhaps she had overreacted a little.

But she couldn't control this constant fear that something might happen to him. She then apologized to others, explaining that the boy had a health problem and wasn't allowed to eat anything with gluten because it would make him sick.

As they walked to the bench where they had left the stroller and the bike, Erik said in a sad voice:

"I wasn't going to take it anyway. I know they have gluten. And I'm not allowed..."

His mother didn't dare say anything to him. What else could she say?

Erik looked around, disappointed, at the children munching on the snacks. He wanted to join in their game, even though his parents had explained to him again and again that it was unhygienic to eat between the slides. His mother offered him a gluten-free snack and asked him to eat it on the bench next to her.

"If you go there, you'll have to share it with them. And we don't have enough for everyone. Eat here, and when you're done, you're free to go play. It's not nice for them to look you in the mouth if you can't give it to them. The little boy chews quickly, with gusto. He'd almost forgotten the incident earlier. But his mother felt her heart breaking for him. 'Can't these kids really keep from eating anywhere, anyway?' she wondered. How much the power of example matters! How easily influenced people are, how greedy..., and how hard it is, as a parent, to teach your child to eat at home, at the table, and not in front of other people. What was the right solution in this situation, she thought?

To teach them both the importance of 3 meals and 2 snacks a day. And to get them used to eating at the table, which is where the expression comes from: to dine, to eat. And for unforeseen situations like this, they will do their best to always have some snacks in their backpack. Because the boy needs to become responsible, to know what is good for him and what is not, so that he can stay with the children even when they eat something he is not allowed to. Play should be more important than food, and parents will make sure to repeat this to them so many times until it is stuck in their minds.

11. AN EXPLANATION IN THE WORDS OF GREAT-GRANDMOTHER

Things have begun to calm down at home, the family has found its rhythm and is slowly getting used to the new lifestyle.

After a few weeks of accommodation, the parents gathered the courage to go on their first visit to their great-grandmother. The trip is meticulously prepared by the parents, who not only make sure they have everything they need for the child, but also prepare themselves mentally for the moment when they will be bombarded with questions from everyone: Where did the illness come from? How long does he have to diet? Why so strict?

"At home everything is easy for us now. On the day we found out the diagnosis, we had our last homemade pizza. I had already promised him we would have pizza for dinner, and we hadn't given up on the idea. It was like a goodbye "feast". From the next day on, we offered him only gluten-free food. We eat the same way he does. We don't buy regular bread in the house anymore, we usually eat without, and if we have something spreadable, like butter or an eggplant salad, then we eat gluten-free baked goods. For sweetness we discovered rice rounds, we ate the best pasta we've ever eaten, made from rice, and I can say we feel really good", says the mother.

"How to eat without bread?" asks great-grandma.

"It's just habit, that's all. Just like when you fast and you know not to eat meat or dairy. That's how we look at it now. It's true that many have criticized our choice, arguing that the diet is strictly for the patient, and that our bodies need gluten grains... That may be so. But it seems inhuman to me to eat in front of my child and have crumbs fall on the table before him, explaining each time why he eats something and we eat something else. He's too young to understand the real reason and I think it's not very high priced to give up for his sake."

"Well, what do we do here?"

"We just ask you not to put all the bread on the table, that's all. Keep your slice in your hand, discreetly, and he'll mind his own business. All this time I've been explaining things to him, he knows that we eat the same as he does, that he's not alone in his struggle, but that others have the right to eat what's good for them. And he seems to get it."

"It's a pity he can't eat some of our country wheat bread", says the great-grandmother. "From now on, we can't even make bread or cakes when he comes here. That's a pity. No more of Grandma's cake trays and piles of doughnuts", the old lady concludes.

"Not necessarily! I brought him new pots and pans especially for him, and if she uses baking paper and gluten-free flour, Grandma can make him something delicious."

"Well, what was wrong with our pots?" asks a puzzled great-grandmother, who holds on to every old tool in her crockery.

"When starting a gluten-free diet, to avoid contamination, it is also recommended to replace pots and pans and especially kitchen utensils. Opinions are divided here. There are voices that say you have to take everything very radically, and other voices that say it's not that serious. I think everyone has to decide for themselves from this point of view. I asked the opinion of the doctor who has us in her care, and she told me: 'It's like when you do a general cleaning. First you take out the bulk, wipe, vacuum, then you deal with the corners and underneath.' Well, initially I replaced the gluten products with the ones gluten-free, then I also replaced some of the pots and pans and cutlery I had in the house. The stainless-steel ones, especially, if you wash them in the dishwasher or hot water, can be used without any problems. On the other hand, anything wooden, plastic or metal joints, such as spoons, choppers, even blenders, graters, all of these clearly need to be replaced, as gluten seems to penetrate well into wood and plastic, as well as through the joints of the tel, mixer and so on. The story of contamination is a complex one. For example, you can contaminate the sick person simply by getting your hands on wheat flour bread and then their food.

Or if there are crumbs of wheat bread on the table. You have to be very careful. The hardest will be when we have to visit someone or eat out, because in a restaurant it can be contaminated very easily. You explain to the waiter about the problem, he passes the information to the kitchen, but because they have a lot of orders, they can take his steak and put it on the plate with the same paddle they used before to put a floured schnitzel or... as it happened to us in the beginning, they brought us 2 pieces of focaccia on the plate next to the food. It's like when you're fasting and they serve you a portion of potatoes and a piece of meat on the same plate."

"Oh! I wouldn't eat off that plate if it was fast day."

"That's what I'm saying. People don't know such details. And they don't know the importance of contamination. I'll admit it took me a long time to figure it out too. At first, I thought the same thing: I put the bread aside and eat, what's the problem? Well, there is... Because the gluten stays there and every trace of gluten matters, no matter how small, even invisible to the naked eye. Gluten once ingested, affects the body of a celiac patient. So since that day when we got focaccia at the restaurant on the same plate as the so-called carefully prepared food, we don't go to the restaurant anymore except with a packet."

"But how can you know if it's been contaminated?"

"A lot of people have asked me this. A lot of people confuse celiac disease... with allergies. They think: someone who has an egg allergy, for example, when they eat an egg product, they get blisters around their mouth or on their body. Let's give him a piece of bread, nothing happens. Well, that's not the case with him. In celiac disease, the small intestine is particularly, but not only, affected. It has little peristyles called villi on the inside, and in Erik's case, when the body comes into contact with gluten, it causes autoimmune reactions in the intestine whereby these villi shrink until they disappear, leading to poor absorption of nutrients from food. This is why he is always iron deficient and anaemic. Because, no matter how much he gets from his diet, if his body is always fighting with gluten, it doesn't function properly and iron is lost. And that's why so many of the usual test values are out of the normal range, unfortunately.

"Sounds pretty bad, dear, what you're saying there! And is the boy doing well if he's on this strict diet?"

"Yes. It's just that we have to stand like a shadow behind him. Good people will want to give him sweets, candy, biscuits. He's still too young, and he can take it enthusiastically. But we must always be there to get his attention, guide and support him. The poor little guy, I've told him so many times about it, that he's obsessed with the idea. I think we've managed to scare him too. He started asking us in the house if the food has gluten. I don't know if he's trying to make sure even here that he's in a safe zone or if it's a test for us, to see if we eat the same way he does."

"Does this have gluten in it?"

"No."

"Does that one? What's that on your plate?"

"That doesn't have any either."

"What about lactose?"

"No. It doesn't have any lactose."

"Good!" then he concludes, victoriously.

"Conversations like this have been happening almost at every meal in our house for a while now. And then, in those moments, I'm confident that I've made the best decision, to eat just like him. What if I had to sit and explain to him at every meal why he isn't eating bread the way we do, or cook two kinds of soup, two kinds of cheesecake and so on. How do I keep his spoon away from my bowl, which he wants to taste, or not contaminate him by putting my hand on one or the other? Only those who don't have children probably imagine that family dinners are still conducted in our home according to the guidelines of the code of good manners... the truth is that we also have quieter meals, especially when the children are asleep, but when they are awake, it is rarely quiet in the kitchen. They want to move from one chair to another, change spoon for spoon, and then eat by hand, but after getting their hands and feet dirty, they realise they weren't even hungry... Erik is delighted to see the little one in his arms. He wants us to spoon-feed him too, to feed him, to let him sit in Mommy's arms, Daddy's arms, and in the baby seat, but then it's like he'll move under the table if the baby gets in there and so on. He's such a little baby. And so innocent! How can I ask him to look in my mouth, eat something in front of him and he'll look long?" wonders the mother. "To help him feel more comfortable with the food issue, I ended up making up all sorts of bedtime stories. His favorite is the one about Eric, the little boy who is gluten-free and faces all sorts of challenges in his daily life."

12. CHILD-FRIENDLY EXPLANATIONS

"Mommy, why all kids are eating something and one isn't?" Erik finally asks, after telling Mom a few stories about his day at the nursery.

"What do you mean?" asks Mom, pretending not to know what he is saying. She's curious to find out what's in his little head and soul, so she can help him better. "Is that what happened at the nursery?" insists the mother.

"Yes. All the children eat something, and one doesn't."

"Who is that one, baby?"

Erik is silent. He doesn't dare articulate a word, and his silence breaks his mother's heart. Darkness falls even harder on the room full of toys. Mother's eyes moisten and she refrains from crying, to keep the noise down. But she feels a lump in her throat, as if she is about to drown. The emotions that wash over her are so contradictory... and she is reminded of the story of the Ugly Duckling, which she had told the child at bedtime a few days ago. She imagined Erik at daycare, sitting alone at the table with his lactose-free yogurt in front of him and thirstily biting into a slice of gluten-free bread. He drools at the others' food, but sits there alone, as if he's being punished. What an ugly picture! Her child, cast aside. He, who used to be in the midst of children, who loved to bite into the neighbor's bread on his way home, who loved cereal with milk and also yogurt... now he sat isolated, alone and sad. For a while now he hasn't been able to count as well as he had learned some time ago. And yet, he did well at this simple equation. It started with one and ended. He didn't have a number two as a consolation, unfortunately. How nice it would be if we knew at least one kid in his situation, to befriend him and see that he wasn't the only one going through this. Maybe he would open his heart before him, share thoughts and experiences in the future and accept everything more easily. Then the mother gets the idea to look for such children. Of course, it's a great idea and I need to get on it as soon as possible. The thought of it makes her come out of her confusion and distress a little and respond to the child.

"Baby, that one's you, right? You don't have to be afraid to admit it! I've already told you what a wonderful child you are. You're very clever to make that remark. And I'll try to answer you whenever you have a question. Well, that baby, meaning you, eats something else because your tummy is a special one that doesn't accept gluten. You're going to ask me why your tummy is special, I know... Because it's God's will. He gives the people He loves dearly some special challenges, and you are a soul who has to overcome that challenge, unfortunately. But you don't have to be sad! Fortunately, technology has come a long way now, so you can eat similar products to those your colleagues eat. It's good at least that there's gluten-free bread or lactose-free yoghurt. Otherwise... I really saw a big problem in this story. But... you shouldn't focus on the food, the focus should be on what comes out of your mouth, i.e., nice words and smiles, as well as your actions, the games you are involved in and so on. I know you'd like to consume exactly what your colleagues have at the table, but unfortunately that's not possible, at least for the moment. And in the long run I hope everything will be fine. Tell me: how do you play with the kids in your group?"

"Nice. With little cars, with little trains, we dance, we sing..."

"This is a great thing. I'm so glad you're having fun. Try to take part in as many activities as possible and put the meal on the back seat. You'll feel much better that way, I promise."

"Yeah, but... why is my tummy special?"

"Because... because that's how life is sometimes" the mother said sadly, noting that all the baby had remembered was this. Then she continues: "You're not the only one in this situation, you're not a freak. I'm sure children can often be mischievous, and in time you'll even find some who will probably offend you. Now I don't know how much of what I'm telling you makes sense to you, but I'm sure we'll come back to the subject at the appropriate time. The point is... don't put everything you hear from others to your heart. A lot of people speak in ignorance. And all we care about is that you're okay. So, concentrate on eating only what you're allowed. You have a whole horizon of products to choose from. You have all your fruit and vegetables, you have dairy products, lactose-free for the moment, admittedly, but you have them, then meat, nuts and even sweets prepared according to special, adapted recipes. Life can still be beautiful. In fact, it is still beautiful. Let's not get bogged down, that is, get stuck in things that can block our energies, that is, make us feel unwell, you know? I told you, you're not the only one in this situation, okay? There's a lot of kids around the world who have to go gluten-free. Or there are some who aren't allowed cow's milk protein at all, or egg, or are allergic to histamine. See, these are challenges! Admittedly, it was better to be perfectly healthy. But the choice wasn't in our hands. So, let's take it all for granted and see what comes out in the end. You know, there's an old saying: what do you do if life gives you oranges?! Let's make lemonade. You want some?"

Silence. Erik had probably been asleep for a while. Mom is wondering if she should feel sorry that he didn't hear her whole story or if it's better that he's settled down and gone to sleep! She'll reflect on the topic and maybe by next time she'll do more research and be inspired to have a better speech.

For now, though, the child's classmates are coming to her mind. And she thinks about how she could teach him to handle their snide remarks better, without turning him into an introvert. 'I remember when I was a kid, and my friends across the block would call me four-eyed stove because I wore glasses. Or that for a whole season I was nicknamed sleepover because I was nicknamed pyjama girl by a friend who noticed while playing leapfrog that I was wearing a pair of tights under my sweatpants because it was cold. For the fun of it, children are willing to make mischievous jokes, not realising how much they can hurt the victim. Nowadays, my friend doesn't remember the nickname with underpants. I reminded her a few years ago and she had no idea she had ever made such a joke. I, on the other hand, remember it like it was the day before yesterday. And I don't want my own child to go through that. Jokes are inevitable. But I do mean that I want him to get his feelings out, to get his anger out and heal from his pain, not to carry around with him inappropriate emotional baggage that shouldn't belong to him, to burden him unnecessarily', the mother reflects.

Parents of children with celiac disease have a responsibility to educate themselves, to know on the one hand the disease and its implications, on the other hand it wouldn't hurt a little nutritional education to support their children to eat nutritionally balanced, taking into account that they remove from their daily diet almost the entire base of the food pyramid. Then they need to learn personal development, to teach the lesson of managing emotions and the importance of life, of finding meaning no matter what. That's why, night after night, Mom makes a habit of telling the bedtime story of Eric, the little boy who wasn't allowed to eat gluten.

"There was once a little boy, Eric, who was almost 3 years old. Eric was the pride of his parents, grandparents and aunt. He was a much-loved little boy, for whom Mommy and Daddy had prayed a lot to God to send him to them. And one day, He took pity on them and sent him to brighten their days...

Eric was spoiled as a child by everyone. Grandma and Grandpa would knead him doughnuts, Mom would make him pizza and all sorts of croissants and pancakes, and he loved to play with flour. When he was little, he used to drag the dining chair over to the kitchen counter, where the "white" operations took place. The little guy would stick his little hands in the soft dough and shape it laughing his mouth off. He would then wipe off the sweat with his little hand and soon turn into a character worthy of Halloween... Mother loved spending time with him and watching him go about his business. Shortly after his 2nd birthday, Eric was introduced to his little brother, Dodo. That's what kids Eric's age called him, unable to pronounce his name. At first, the little boy was excited by the baby's presence, who sat quietly in his crib and slept a lot. The mother kept telling him that she would come home with him at some point, and that she would have to breastfeed him, as she had done with him as a baby. Mom remembers that when Eric was a baby, everyone would watch him sleep, count his breaths, and jump up and down when he opened his eyes. This baby, however, sleeps alone in the bedroom with the door closed, and they are only concerned with giving him the bare necessities so that they have as much time left for Eric as possible.

"And when does he leave?" little Eric asked one day.

"Who's supposed to leave?" said the woman, very surprised.

"The baby!"

"Go where?" said the mother. "He's not going away. He'll stay with us forever, like you." It was only at that moment Mom realized that Eric had just had an... awakening (i.e., he had just realized something). Until then he either hadn't been bothered by the baby's existence, or hadn't realized that from now on everything was split two ways. That's why Mom was trying to spend more and more time with Eric. They would read stories, build lego castles, race cars or play pizza. But the child was eager for his own age, so his parents decided to take him to daycare...

"And did he like daycare? What do you think?" asked Erik's mother, interrupting Eric's story for a moment.

"I think he liked it", said the little boy. "And what else did this child do?"

"As his little brother grew older and needed to be carried around, Eric began to get jealous, and Mom was finding it harder and harder to divide them. Eric was an intelligent and very determined child. At nursery he slept alone at lunchtime, without a bottle, and at home he demanded to go to sleep only with his mother and a bottle of goat's milk. But from time to time, night after night, he began to get tummy aches. And it hurt so bad, so bad that he would wake up from sleep and roll around on the carpet in pain."

"Like me?" Erik interrupted the story this time.

"Unfortunately, yes."

"And what did he do to make them go away? Was he taking the syrups?"

"His parents did some tests, and the doctor recommended that he go exclusively gluten-free. So for a while now, he's been eating only gluten-free products. And he's happy his tummy doesn't hurt anymore."

"It doesn't hurt me now either", Erik says.

"I'm very happy. It's great that you're okay! So, what would you think if we go to sleep?" asked Mother. "That way, tomorrow you'll wake up refreshed and be able to play a lot. And then, just like today, you can collect your toys yourself. I appreciate that you understand that this is your job" said Mom, kissing him gently on the forehead to say goodnight.

13. ERIK REFUSES TO SLEEP

After the evening meal, Erik goes to the bathroom with Dad, and Mom stays to clear the table. Most evenings, they do this together and use the time in the kitchen to catch up on what happened during the day, who did what, share impressions, catch up on the day's highlights and plan their next day. Tonight, however, Erik is very tired and goes to the bathroom early. Dodo stays with Mom until she puts the dishes in the washing machine, and to give Erik some time to get in the tub. He is then also taken out of the stool, which he has started to climb, and taken to the bathroom.

"Come on, you little donut! Come here. Will you put him in the tub with me? Erik asks excitedly. I want to take a bath with him, I do. Come on, come here, little one." Whether he understands what his big brother is saying or does it on his own initiative, the little guy desperately pulls the bodysuit off and tries to perch on the tub. It's one of the happiest moments of the day, as the two of them play in the tub, splashing and laughing their heads off.

"Nooo. That's my toy. Give it to me. Give it to me now!" cries Erik, breaking the family's silence after Dodo has honored his invitation and reached into the tub beside him. The parents try to reconcile them, dividing the toys by age, but they don't always want to play with what's given to them. Of course, the objects in the other's hand are more interesting, even if he had shown no interest in them before.

"Come on" said Dad, pacifying. "You must learn to share! It's not okay to snatch the toy out of his hand just because you're older. You're stronger than him now, but there will come a day when he'll get stronger too, and I'd don't like to see you fighting side by side. Remember what Mommy told you about toys?"

"Yeah. But I want it", said the baby.

"Doesn't the rule say that the one who gets it has priority, and the next must either ask for it nicely, or wait for it to be put down? I thought he took it first, if I saw correctly."

"Yes, but... give it to me!" insists Erik, snatching the toy from his little brother's hand, who starts crying. Mom eventually makes up, but she's not happy about it.

"Look, he's younger and you're lucky he calms down quickly, the little fellow is content with what he's given. Right now, we're happy that he calms down right away, but in the long run you know I'm not going to encourage him to give up... I don't want him to always lose, to have the spirit of a loser. Besides, you can't call yourself a winner either simply because your opponent backed down and gave you the thing. It's not the right time for theory right now, but one thing I can tell you: I don't like you doing this and I don't encourage you to do it anymore! I still love you no matter what you do, but I dislike your behavior in these situations."

Mom finishes washing little brother and takes him out of the bathroom. Dad takes Erik out and both kids go through the ritual of getting dressed, which leaves with squealing, playful, naked and running around.

"My goodness, how you've activated! You look very sleepy. Come on, let's put your shirt on. How long do I have to chase you?"

"I don't want to. I'll stay naked a little longer", said the baby, tumbling around the bed and bouncing between the pillows.

"Come on, five minutes and we're done. It's quite late. We have to get to sleep, we're up early tomorrow."

"No, no. I'm still playing."

"Come on, darling, look, Dodo wants to go to bed. Let me get him ready for bed."

"Why does he sleep alone?" Erik asked.

Mom looked at him and said:

"So, I can sleep with you. Or... do you want to sleep alone too?"

"No, no, no. I sleep with you, with you", Erik repeated, as if his mother didn't understand.

"Well, then, go to your room and stay there quietly. Look, Daddy's waiting for you for the evening game."

"Is he preparing milk for me?"

"Come on, please! Stop blabbing! You've been stirring the bath tonight. Go to Daddy's and give me time to put the boy to sleep so I can come to you later. Otherwise, none of you will fall asleep and we'll all be up at midnight."

"Daddy, can you put me some cartoons?" Erik shouted from the hall.

"No" said Mom, while closing the bedroom door. "You've already watched cartoons today, sorry. The doctor said no more than half an hour of screen time, accumulated over the day. Tomorrow, we'll gladly accommodate you within the time limit. Go ahead, read a story or do whatever else you want, but in silence."

After putting Dodo to sleep, Mother came to the big boy's room.

"Ready, is he asleep?" Erik asked curiously. "So soon?"

"Yes. So fast" said Dad, as if imitating him. "So should you. Look, it's so simple: put your head on the pillow, stare at the wall, listen to the story or think of something nice and close your eyes."

"Come on, you should try it" says dad to mom. "Today he doesn't want to sleep with me under any circumstances."

Mom sighs. 'He doesn't want to sleep at all, it's not that he doesn't want to sleep with you,' she said softly, as if she were speaking just for herself.

"Come on, sweetie. We'll turn off the night light now, too. It's time to sleep."

"But I'm not sleepy! And I don't want you to turn off the light. I can't see you anymore. Please!"

"But you don't have to see me in order to sleep, baby! I'm here with you. Look, give me your hand and close your eyes. What would you like us to do to make it easier for you to fall asleep and sleep better? Did Daddy tell you the story?"

"Yes, he did. And he gave me a massage. But I want you too. Tell me a story. I want Eric's story, please!"

"Well, honey, I'm tired too. Do you want me to tell you The Three Little Pigs or Little Red Riding Hood or just close our eyes and go to sleep?"

"Come on, tell me the story with Eric, so I can get some sleep, please. What did he do?"

"There once was a little boy, Eric was his name. And he was a very clever, happy, playful child. He was 2 and a bit when his little brother came into the world, and his mother had to divide her time between him and the baby. In order not to resent the little one and not to feel that his presence affected him in any way, the mother made an effort to spend a lot of time with the big boy. While the baby slept, they played with toy cars, built towers, read stories, drew pictures and romped around the house. When he was very small, the baby's presence was hardly felt in the house. But he did have his moments, when something upset him and he cried, and his mother had to carry him. Erik walked back and forth, holding onto her leg. And one day he asked:

'When does he leave from us?'

'Who should leave?'

'The Baby...'

Then the mother became worried, realizing that jealousy was beginning to set in between the two brothers. She did her best not to let Eric feel his place threatened by the little one. He got lots of toys and attention, even the baby toys, but as the little one grew, so did Eric, and the mother thought it was time to explain things better between the two of them. Once Dodo starts to walk on his own two feet, he'll explore around the house and investigate toys too. This desire for exploration should not be suppressed, because what a child learns in the early years is very important. If he is always told that he has to give toys, even his own, when someone asks him to, he will become resigned and will not have a word to say. This will be the case later in life, and this is not quite ok. Because people have to defend their rights and beliefs. We have to talk a lot among ourselves and come to an agreement when we get into a conflict area. We have to come to an agreement from which everyone gains as much as possible. Not one to emerge victorious and the other defeated. Because, okay, if you're the winner, that's fine. But if you put yourself in the loser's shoes, and stay there every time, how would you feel? It's important that every time you want something or take an action, you think about the consequences and how others will feel... If you need to, think more than once before you act. Let's think about something very familiar to you: when you go to the park and see a nice toy belonging to a child, would you like to get your hands on it too?'

'Yes'

'Well, that's what you have to keep in mind when someone takes a toy from you or when you snatch the toys from Dodo's hand: how does he feel at that moment? And how do you feel when someone doesn't give you something. Or when they take your things without asking. I'm not saying you have to give every toy to everyone. Far from that thought. But when you go out with toys, for example, keep in mind that you have to take a toy with you that you are willing to share, put it on the table for others to touch... Otherwise, others will get frustrated that they don't have one, and that means we're not doing a good thing.'

"But Daddy's never giving away his car" Erik interrupted the story.

"I totally agree. So, you have found yourself in the story, said Mom smiling ... It's your right not to give. And it's not okay to give stuff to anyone, either, like I said. But Daddy doesn't mind if someone touches the car, or if he positions himself next to it to take a closer look. That's what it's all about. Don't be brutish when you refuse. The kid in front of you doesn't just have to hear it: NO. It's my favorite toy, and I can't give it to you. But I'll let you have it, and you can analyze it all you want. That's fine with me. You don't have to run, sulk or cry! Will there be children who won't understand and insist? Of course, they will. Many will. But you will stand firm if you still don't want to give it, and you will politely refuse. I can't give it to you, but you can ... whatever you want to let him do. But back to the story..."

'For a while, Eric starts to act nicer, because his mother kept explaining how nice it feels to share, that he has to do it with all his heart, with joy, just like when he gets something. Because when you give away from little that you have, the one next to you is happy, and it charges you up positively too. Do you know what that means? It means he practically overwhelms you with his positive energy, his smile and his gratitude, and you can be happy that you have helped. You know what I mean?'

Mom lifts her head slightly and notices that the little boy is finally asleep. She would however have liked for him to have heard the end of the story, but there is still another day tomorrow. The clock strikes almost midnight, and the baby still wakes up many times during the night, so it's time for her to sleep too. 'Good night, children! God bless you!'

14. POLITENESS AND PAMPERING IN THE COMFORT OF HOME

"Mommy, can you explain to me again why Dodo doesn't poop in the potty?" he asked one evening. Mom wasn't so much impressed by his curiosity as by the way he asked the question.

Erik is speaking more and more correctly and becoming more polite every day. He amazed her with his behaviour even during the day. For example, when they went out to the park, Erik asked permission to go to the litter bin, which was further away from the bench they were sitting on, to throw a napkin. Being in the park, and having a direct view of him... the mother didn't think it was dangerous to leave him alone, but the child appreciated her approval and made a point of mentioning it:

"Thank you, Mommy. Thank you for letting me go to the trash alone."

Then she thought of the other times when it looked like Erik was being too polite. Most of the time, she was glad he did. Sometimes, though, it seemed a little too formal. There was no need to thank her for letting him throw a napkin in the trash. Right now, her mind was working at maximum capacity. She wondered which was worse, which terrified him more: the limits placed on how far away from her he could be when they were out of the house, or the polite formalities? Although it was more the last ones that he simply borrowed from his parents' vocabulary. Whenever they do something wrong to him, they usually apologise. Thus, the child has learned it is okay to offer apologies at any time. Grown-ups can make mistakes too, not just little ones, and everyone needs to admit their mistake when it's appropriate, own it and think about what they can learn from it. That way, mistakes can be avoided in the future.

"Come on! You don't talk to me anymore, what are you doing?" the child suddenly asked. I'm not sleepy yet. "I want you to tell me something else. Or play a little!"

"Excuse me! My mind went somewhere else. I'm just here with you now. But I regret to inform you, Mr. Erik, that it's very late and we're not turning on the light to play. I'll take you in my arms and... good night, baby!"

"Please, come on, a short story! Whatever you want!" begs the little boy.

"Okay. Look, once upon a time there was a little boy about three years old, around your age, extremely polite. During the day, when he was playing with his little brother, who was 1 year old, he would play all sorts of pranks, invent games and act like a baby to get his mother's attention, even though she always told him she loved him even though he had grown up and was no longer a baby. Despite his mischief at home, the little boy grew smarter and more polite every day, and his parents were very proud of him. They thanked God every day for sending them such great joy. The two children are their sunshine. And they love them no matter what they do, even when they argue, hit each other or shove each other."

"I also quarrel with Dodo" Erik said...

"Yes. I know! But it's not something I enjoy, you know, neither me, nor Daddy. We're your parents and we love you no matter what you do or how you are. To us, you're the most wonderful children in the world. That's how all children are to their parents. That's why it makes me sad when you fight or hurt each other. I wish those moments would go away, that you would always get along. Siblings are ideal to be friends as well, especially since you are close in age and will be able to go to different activities together later on or go to the same friendship groups."

"Sibling power!" shouts the child, imitating his favourite cartoon heroes!

"That's right. Sibling power. Sometimes cartoons are good too, you learn something educational. But come on, we've been going on and on. I suggest you close your eyes and go to sleep. Tomorrow's a new day."

"Yeah, it is. And we're going to kindergarten. I like it because there are lots of kids to play with. Even if we don't all eat the same... And we have little cribs, like a baby's crib, where we sleep. At home, why can't I sleep in a crib?"

"Because I wouldn't have space next to you" laughed the mother. "If you want to sleep alone, I'll get you a crib right away" she pretended.

"No. No. I sleep with you. I don't want to be in the crib anymore" he added, curling his hands behind her neck to make sure she stayed there.

Mom wanted to explain a little more about meals at the

daycare, but she didn't want to prolong the discussion, as it was already late.

"Then quiet, please! I'm sleepy!"

15. IRON SUPPLEMENTS RESTORE HIS APPETITE

"Grandma, is it ready, my sweet honey tea?"

"Grandma's not here anymore", said Dad, who had immediately appeared in front of the bedroom door.

"But where is she?"

"She's gone home."

"Why? Why did she go home?"

"Because... because that's what people do: they come to visit, stay a few days, then go to their house. We do the same thing when we visit them."

"But why can't she stay here?"

"Because she has her own house."

"And why does she have her own house?"

"Hm..." said his father, thinking that he wouldn't be able to get away with it. Their "why" discussions could go on for an hour. "Tell me, why do you like it when Grandma's here?"

"Because I like it that way."

"But why do you like it that way? Can you think of an example?"

"I like it when we go to the park and she makes me a cup of tea with lots of honey..." Erik makes a long face, then continues: "She promised to make me tea, and toast with butter, and a soft egg... but she left..."

"That's all right, you wolf-hungry boy. We'll settle this over breakfast. We'll fix anything you want. I'm so glad you're hungry."

"It's about time" Mother said, stepping up to them. "The iron supplements we're giving him are beginning to have effect. Otherwise, the anaemia always weakens his strength and his appetite goes. That's right: Did you know that after we give him this new iron supplement, he has to be active getting such a high dose? I admit I didn't know, no one told me until now. It was only the Ear, Nose and Throat doctor that came out with the information, and thank goodness it did, because I often gave him the drops in the evening, close to bedtime."

"That's right. There are so many facts unknown in his condition, that we have to be up all the time with our ears up and screens on, who knows what more information comes out. Let's be healthy, and we'll take it all in stride."

"Speaking of which..." says the mother, "have you managed to approach the subject of 'just one no' from the nursery? It seems to me that frustration is already arising from the restrictions. I don't know how to proceed better: take him home before lunch, avoid him looking at his classmates' plates? Because he has to go to the collective. His social and educational needs must be met, there is no question of withdrawing him. I understand there was a child with the same problem in daycare once before and he dropped out."

"Possibly. The issue of contamination in mixed kitchens is very controversial. The risk is particularly high. Realistically, I don't think anyone is going to sit there and prepare his meal specifically, when they have hundreds of menus to cook."

"You're right. But he has a right to scholarship, as you said. And it's not his fault he has this nasty disease. I also understand the system. But what did we do wrong? What's his fault for choosing such a fragile body? His belly is always swollen, despite his diet, I don't know what to do. We really have to be careful about everything. And especially his medication. Apparently, many syrups, and even powdered medicines, contain gluten."

"Can I have a syrup, Mommy?"

"No, baby."

"Why not? You were saying something about sweets..."

"Because it' not the time for them right now. I was talking to Daddy about something else, it's not time for syrup. They're given on doctor's orders, I know you like them because they're sweet, but you mustn't abuse them. Otherwise, they won't work.

If you want something sweet, you can always have fruit at the moment." She didn't finish talking, because suddenly remembered what a doctor had taught her earlier, that one shouldn't abuse fruit either. It would be better to be more careful about the time of day when you offer it to him. Ideally, they should be eaten in the first part of the day, about 1-2 hours away from the meal, just like in the nursery programme. Because when he eats fruit in the evening or immediately after a meal it makes the digestion process more difficult, and as his intestines are already inflamed due to illness, they should not burden him with anything else. She remembers how much he used to love steaming apples when he was younger. So, she suggests she makes him one now, and soon the heady smell of baked apple, sprinkled with cinnamon, wafts through the air.

16. KINDERGARTEN... WITH INTOLERANCE TO GO

"It's time, my precious!" said Mom, touching him gently on the back.

Erik stretches out like a sleepy cat and asks, eyes closed:

"Time for what?"

"For going to the kindergarten", said Mom. 'To throw you into the fierce clutches of society, and of people who are unwilling to protect you despite my desperate prayers', she thought, as she stroked his little legs further and encouraged him with kisses. The summer vacation passed quickly, and settling into kindergarten was proving difficult. He had barely gotten used to the nursery's schedule and teachers, now he had to start all over again. Mom felt sorry for him, having to wake him up, especially when he was sleeping so nice and deeply.

"Come on. I've packed your lunch. The teacher's waiting for you and your tea's getting cold. Please, baby, stop stalling. Look, I'll make your morning a little more pleasant, shall I?"

Mom carries him to the bathroom, where she helps him wash

his hands and face.

"You got me wet, Erik protests. I don't want you to get me wet. Leave me alone!"

"Of course, I got you wet", laughed Mom. "How else could I help you? To wash, you have to get wet. Come on, let's brush your teeth and get dressed quickly or we'll be late."

"Okay, but I'll hold the toothbrush and brush myself, okay?"

"Of course, you do. I'm really glad to hear that. But promise not to swallow the toothpaste, okay?"

"Sure", laughed the little boy, handing his mother the empty toothbrush. Look!

"We're not even done talking" Mom pretended to be angry.

"Come on, you know it's gluten-free paste... It's good," he said, to soften her up.

"I know it's flavored, but it's good for brushing teeth, not for eating. All right, let's hurry up a bit, or else the kindergarten doors are closing."

"Is Dodo up yet?"

"He's still sleeping."

"Well, shouldn't we take him too? Let's leave him at home, Erik said seriously."

"How can we leave him at home? How would you feel if I went somewhere with him and you were left alone in the house?"

"Well... I wouldn't like it."

"See? Then he wouldn't like it either. Before you do or say anything, please put yourself in the other person's position. There's a saying: What you don't like, someone else doesn't like either."

"What is a proverb?"

"A proverb? Well," said Mom, "a proverb is a sentence, a phrase that expresses a teaching born of people's experience. Something that often turns out to be true and can be a piece of advice."

"I understand. All right, then, if we're taking him, I want you to dress him first."

"Really? How did you come up with that idea?" Mom asked,

more for the art of conversation.

"I thought so. Here, in my head. Isn't that nice?"

"Yes, it's very good that you think. It's just... now it's time for you to get dressed. Dodo's almost ready, I dressed him while he was sleeping, I'll just put his hoodie on when we get ready to walk out the door."

"Then can I have some biscuits? Some of mine."

"Mommy, there are no cookies of mine or yours. There are only crackers and gluten-free crackers. And you know which ones your tummy needs, which ones are good for her, right?"

"The gluten-free ones."

"Good. Good job. Come on now, let's get moving! I'll never be done talking to you!"

The mother takes the half-adorned little boy in her arms, covers him with a blanket and puts him in the stroller. She puts on Erik's shoes, who is still talking like a broken windmill, and signals him to go out the door.

"Now we're all ready. But I want to be in the stroller. Put me in it. I beg you!"

Mom doesn't want to tease him any more early in the morning. She's already woken him up with difficulty, the little one gets up in his seat too and starts to squirm, so he complies.

"I'll sit you down as soon as I get down the stairs, please! You know it's harder to lift the trolley down the steps with both of you on it. Someday it'll break if we overload it. And my back will break..."

Erik complies, opens the door to the elevator, they all get off and head for the stables, both of them in the stroller, behaving themselves, busy munching on a gluten-free cookie. Mom enjoys a few moments of quiet while the two little mouths are occupied with the cookies. Kindergarten is a block from the house. Erik knows the way well, for next to it is his favorite tree, where he has done most of his climbing since he was a little boy.

"I don't want to go!" he breaks the silence at last.

"What do you mean?" asked Mom, who felt her heart leap out of her chest. "How can you not want to? Well, didn't we say that at kindergarten you'll have fun, you'll make lots of friends, you'll play with lots of toys other than the ones we have at home? Besides, you'll do activities with the lady and you'll learn new things, and at the end you'll tell me about it, so we can teach Dodo too."

"I don't want to learn."

"Why not?" asked Mom, surprised.

"I don't. I don't want to go."

Mom pushes the cart with hurried steps, looking at the clock. There's plenty of time. Still, will he reconsider by the time they get in, or will he make a real scene at the entrance again! He remembers with horror the day before, when he had taken it with difficulty from the baby carriage. Dodo also wanted to jump out of the cart and couldn't cope with them both. She had left the little one by the cart, in his socks, trying to pick up Erik, who was clinging tightly to the cart with both hands. By this time Dodo had hurried off down the driveway, towards a windmill, through the crowd of parents bringing their children to kindergarten. Mom then ran after him, to retrieve him, and Erik got his ass back in the cart and gripped his hands even tighter, fighting back, resisting her desperate prayers to get out and go inside. She remembered how sick she had felt then, how cold shivers ran through her entire body and beads of sweat rolled down her back, down her shirt. She could hardly keep off from crying. She wanted to turn around and take him home, but that wasn't an option. It was enough to set a precedent, as had happened in so many other situations, and then Erik would be tied to the job forever. No, she had to find a solution to convince him. Her mind was working fast, but the child had curled up like a clam in its shell. He was there, but he didn't seem to hear anything. All he kept saying was: 'No, I don't want to, Mommy I want to stay with you.' And the mother's soul crumbled, crumbled... She looked around desperately for help, for anyone's help, but she had to find it in herself, she had to dig for the power to solve the problem. And now she thought with horror that she would go through something similar today. Mother tried to pull herself together, took a deep breath and prepared herself for what was to come.

"Come on, maybe it's your lady at the door this time" she tried to cheer him up.

"No!" Erik replies, seriously.

And when they got to the door, she was horrified to find that there were other children crying, and the more they gathered, the more Erik became agitated and resonated with their condition.

"Look, Ilinca, Theodore! Come on, your classmates are in. Give me a kiss and go with them" she tried again.

"I don't want to!"

"It's hard to settle in" whispered the mother in a low voice.

The surrounding parents agreed with her, each trying to console and persuade their own child to step over the kindergarten gates, while the ladies waited smiling and with open arms to welcome anyone else willing to enter the classroom.

"I'll come and get you quickly" the mother called out from the doorway after finally entering. And she kept her word. At noon she rushed through the gate, among the first parents. Erik was playing merrily among the children and spotted her late, when she was already close to them. He came excitedly to the fence of the playground where they were being taken out after their midday nap and shouted:

"Mommy, you came!"

"Of course, I came. Isn't that what we agreed!"

According to the teacher, once in the classroom, the children quickly forget their anger. They concentrate on changing their shoes, make another joke, wash their hands and hurry off to the table. Too bad parents don't have this quick reboot system, and can't get their minds off the angry little mice that walk across the kindergarten doorstep all day. But as someone said, children don't stay angry for long. And that's a wonderful thing. Sweet, innocent creatures that you are!

At home, the mother tries to connect with the child, to see what hidden, unsuspected emotions might be affecting him so much that he does NOT want to go to kindergarten.

"What do you like there?" she asked him.

"The horses on wheels, which are bigger than my Chiufi."

Mother looked at him in wonder. Chiufi was a pretty big swinging horse. How big were those wheeled horses? Anyway... the important thing was that he'd found something he liked that would keep him busy there.

"But WHAT don't you like?"

"That they have big cups... And they have TVs with ugly cartoons."

How much of it is reality and how much is science fiction, God knows. But one thing's for sure. It would be great if educators and teachers could get closer to his heart and help him befriend the kids better, so he could go to kindergarten for pleasure. In addition to all this, perhaps it would be useful, in all educational institutions, to introduce lessons about children with food allergies and intolerances into the curriculum. It is important that other children understand the condition of the sick person, perhaps there are times when they too crave something from them, not just the other way around. But at the same time, they should all be aware of how much harm it could do to them if they were to offer them a gluten product... Children can often act out of love, generosity or impulse. But they need to be aware of the seriousness of such an act. Because their body struggles for months to recover from contamination, whether intentional or accidental. While she was thinking about all this, the mother came up with the idea of suggesting to the teacher that she gives such a lesson one day.

17. ANGER, FRUSTATION, SADNESSTHE

"You can play for another 10 minutes and then collect your toys! It' s time to get ready for dinner" says Daddy.

But Erik pretends not to hear him. He continues to roll the cars across the carpet, grinding noisily through his teeth: blum, bllum. Dodo imitates him with his little vehicle, shouting at the top of his voice: bum, bum. The parent watches them play with pleasure, after a short while reminding them that Mom is almost ready with dinner.

"You have about 5 minutes left and that's it. Look, since he's little and can't pick up toys yet, I'll help you instead. That way he'll see us working as a team and he'll learn how to do it too."

"I don't want to," said the little boy, seriously.

"What do you mean, you don't want to?"

"I don't. Leave me alone!" he added, reinforcing what he had said.

"I don't want to. I can't. Leave me alone. I'll do what I want, when I want. I eat what I want and how I want. I don't want with you, I want with Daddy, or the other way around..." are phrases that Erik has been repeating more and more lately, and that his parents don't like to hear. Although they keep getting his attention, the little boy continues to use them. Desperate about his behaviour, they keep explaining to him that it's wrong for him to behave like this, but he doesn't seem to understand.

"Okay" Dad approves him, calming down, thinking it won't do any good to get angry at this point. Then he continues: "here's how we do it, you know there's a schedule we follow in our daily activities. There's a time for everything: for sleeping, for eating, for bathing and for playing... now we have to get ready for dinner, whether you like it or not. Look, I'll give you five more minutes, even though I'm hungry because I'm back from work. When the time is up, you have two choices: you can pick up the toys and put them back, or you can leave them spread out like that, but when I pick them up, Mommy and I reserve the right to do whatever we want with them. We'll confiscate them. What's it gonna be?"

Erik stares at Dad. There was no trace of a smile on his face, no sign of reconciliation. He knew he was serious, so he began to gather up the toys and put them back in the basket, grumbling. Then, seeing that dad was no longer willing to help him as he had originally offered, he begged, looking him in the eye:

"Will you help me?"

Father felt sorry for him and answered his request in the affirmative. He thought perhaps he was too young to be asked to do such things. Maybe he was being too hard on him... but no, it's not an ideal age for that. He's also sick, and he's had enough of it... Hm, these are elementary, common-sense things though, and as he gets used to it at a young age, he'll do it when he gets older. He needs to learn from now on to take care of things, to put them away, order will help him in any situation.

After lunch, the children continued their play on the kitchen carpet, while parents took the opportunity to discuss the issue.

"Surely he heard someone at the kindergarten talking like that!" the two adults agreed. Until recently, the child hadn't misbehaved, nor was he outraged at anyone, whether it was revenge.

"Is it possible that something is going on there that we don't know about?" Dad wondered one evening.

"Or maybe he's imitating a colleague", Mom said. "Remember when a child at the nursery didn't eat the peppers in the soup and then he started investigating all the ingredients on the plate and started making us put all the vegetables away? I think something similar is happening now. I thought the ladies said they had some difficulty with children talking back."

"Oh. That's exactly what we needed!" Dad thought, disappointed and tired after a long and tiring day at work. "Tomorrow we really need to have a serious talk with him. It's not right what's happening. We're giving him a lot of cravings because he's disadvantaged in some way, to make up for what he lacks, but that doesn't mean we have to allow him to behave badly. It's essential that we educate him properly and teach him that there are limits. Besides, this will help him in the future in every way. Come on, everybody to bed now!"

"How did my hero wake up this morning? Are you ready for a great weekend day?" That's how Dad greeted him first thing Saturday morning, as soon as he opened his eyes. "Come on, let's go to the bathroom before you wet the bed!" he said, smiling friendly and massaging his lazily stretching legs.

"I don't want to!" Erik said.

"You don't? What's that supposed to mean?" asked the adult, as he massaged him in a friendly manner.

"I don't want to'" Erik continued.

"I understand. But I don't know what you mean by that" continued Dad, insistently. "Why don't you? I mean... it would help me understand if you explained. You don't want to because you don't need to go to the toilet, or because you're lazy, or maybe you need help... What this is about."

"Yeah. I don't really feel like doing it right now."

"And you think if I wait five, ten minutes, you might still go?"

"I don't know."

"Are you still thinking?"

"Okay. I'm trying."

"Then... while you're thinking about it, I suggest we go over our family's morning rules. So, what do we do when we get up first thing in the morning?"

"We lie down... And eat. And, uh, can I get some cartoons?"

"Nice try, young man. But it doesn't work that way with me. And don't worry, time's running out and the ten minutes are up, and you're still going to the bathroom, you're not going to pee yourself, are you? So, in the morning, after lying in bed like a four-foot cat, you go to the bathroom to wash your hands, face and teeth. You take a leak and wash your hands one more time before getting out of the bathroom. Oh, and don't forget to flush. I've seen it happen! Then you change out of your pyjamas and report to the kitchen. Mom will sometimes receive you in your pyjamas, but never unwashed or, worse, with wet pants. So come on! Time's up and I hope I don't hear another 'I don't want to' now."

"But why not?"

"Because you didn't choose the right context. I'm sure you heard somewhere or someone say 'I don't want to', but I don't think you paid much attention to what they meant. For example, it's perfectly normal to want or not want to play with a toy car, to want the green blouse instead of the red one, or other things that don't affect anyone else around you, that only affect you and improve your mood. Okay. I understand saying you don't want to even when it comes to food. Although then it would be more appropriate to say 'thanks, I'm not hungry now, I'll eat later'. Or 'I don't like this, if you can, please offer me something else or I'd prefer to be able to eat something else now'. You can't say you don't want to wash. That is an obligation and we don't discuss it. It's like saying you want to go naked outside. That's not appropriate."

"What do you mean naked?"

"I mean... naked. Without any clothes."

"That would amuse my friends terribly, and everyone I meet. But I'd be very ashamed."

"I'm glad you understand. Well, then, do you have any objection to brush your teeth?"

"Yes, I do. Why do I always have to brush them?"

"It's a good point. And I'm sorry you don't do it all the time. It's necessary to brush your teeth for several reasons: for example, in the morning your mouth smells bad because of the secretions from your stomach that go up your oesophagus during the night. And brushing will freshen your breath. Your mouth will smell nice, which will make you feel better overall. Then, most importantly, you'll have clean, hygienic teeth, residue leads to decay over time."

"Good. But I read in a book with my mom that it's not so bad to go to the dentist."

"Of course, it's not. But if you get early caries your teeth will be affected and it will be harder to keep your teeth until old age. And with implanted teeth, believe me it's more complicated to eat anything. It will never be the same again. You've seen how Grandpa struggles, and how much time he spends at the doctor's. Come on, it's better to care, to prevent, than to treat. Especially since your health problem has some impact on your teeth. Unfortunately, your new lifestyle can also have an impact on your tooth enamel. So, I say it's not that much effort compared to how much good brushing our teeth can do. Are we clear?"

"Okay, Daddy. Now can I have some biscuits, please?"

"Uh, only if you promise to brush your teeth right after you eat them. I thought that was the rule you and Mommy made, wasn't it? You brush your teeth after every sweet snack."

"Fine. Fine. Come on, give me! Yay!"

"Have you discussed the matter?" Mom asked curious.

"Yes" Dad said. "We discussed like boys. Right, champ?"

"Uh, huh" Erik said through his teeth, nodding as he munched on the round gluten-free biscuits.

"You still have to talk about 'leave me alone!'" said Mom, following her husband around the house. "Maybe you can bring that up."

"Let's take them one at a time" he said calmly. "It's possible that he often feels really trapped by all our demands, all the pressure we put on him. He needs time to assimilate all the information, and space. And sometimes we do invade it" he completes.

"That's pretty much it. Plus, he's got the same old problem with Dodo. He either wants to stay in his crib, or he calls him into his room, or he kicks him out, or he gives him a toy, then snatches it out of his hand because it's his, and so on. Then we get into the sensitive area with feeding, this you can, that you can't, and he probably feels overwhelmed by so many things."

"Let's take things one by one. And if you patiently explain everything to him, he understands. He's not a bad kid. He's not even bad when he has tantrums. Surely, he has some unfulfilled need. We're too tired to search, and he doesn't know how to manage his emotions, he feels overwhelmed and has to express himself somehow. Come on, it'll be fine. Keep your spirits up!"

18. IN A 3-YEAR-OLD'S MIND: "WHY AM I DIFFERENT?"

"What a beautiful belly you have!" Mother shouted, watching him struggle to get dressed.

Delighted by the comment, the little boy lifted the blouse he had just managed to put on so that his mother could admire his belly. He puffed himself up like a small turkey and approached her:

"Is she pretty?" he asked.

"It's the most beautiful tummy." Mom kissed him on the belly and took him in her arms. She squeezed him tightly to her chest and gently undressed him.

"It's good she's not bloated anymore, isn't it?" Erik asked, to his mother's astonishment.

"It's wonderful. Don't you feel better now?"

"Yes. I'm fine."

"Does your tummy still hurt?

"No" he said, breathing in and out sharply, swelling in his belly, then showing his flat abdomen again.

"I'm so glad you're okay. That's all that matters, after all, despite any sacrifice."

"Yeah, but... what did the doctor say? When will I be able to eat lactose?"

"Technically, the doctor gave her permission for you to have lactose. It just doesn't seem to me to be good for you yet, so I'd prefer to eat it only occasionally. I mean... she didn't forbid it, but as a precaution, we're still on a diet."

"What about gluten? When can I eat gluten?"

"Well..." said Mom, and a lump went down her throat as her eyes clouded over. "When researchers discover a drug that can allow you to eat gluten, probably. Not at the moment."

"Why not right now?"

"Because it's not good for your tummy. You know I've explained what happens in the body when you have an autoimmune condition. And in this case, the body sees gluten as an enemy and attacks it, destroying the villi in the small intestine first."

"But is Dodo's tummy good for him?"

"Oh, sweetie. You're asking these questions... It's not bad for him, it's true. But look, for instance, he's not allowed any hot peppers. And he doesn't eat salt. Nor honey, which you like very much... He has his own restrictions. No need to compare yourself to anyone. You're wonderful just the way you are. Learn to value yourself beyond all restrictions. We need to be thankful that we're fine just the way we are. And pray every day for health."

"Yeah, but... why is my tummy like that, Mommy?"

"It's God's will, honey."

But why did God want it that way? Why did he want it that way?

Mommy took a long pause. All sorts of thoughts were running through her mind. Images of healthy children, eating whatever they wanted, from whatever store, were flashing before her eyes. Her heart was pounding in her chest and a powerful rage was raging inside her: God is unfair, she thinks. He has punished my poor child. God, what harm have I done, and to whom, that you punished us all like this? Then she thinks of other children, very ill, who may never see the light of day again. And her heart stops its gallop slightly.

"Let's thank Him that you're okay the way you are, baby! There are sicker children in this world. The important thing is that we can keep the illness under control by diet. I know it's hard, sweetheart, but together we'll get through anything. I promise. God, you see..., He sends us one of these trials to see how strong we are. We don't have to turn against Him. On the contrary. Let's draw near, pray every day and have hope. He gave the sickness, only He can guide us to face it."

"Is he that powerful?"

"He's powerful as you can't even imagine."

"And has He done all that we see?"

"Absolutely."

"But how did He know how to do all this?"

"Because He is the biggest and most important. He is the Lord of the world and of us all. And whatever needs or desires we have; we must turn to Him. The same when we are wrong. And let us never forget on any day to thank Him for all He has given us."

"Why should we thank Him?"

"Because it is only by His will that we have all that we have. He leads us, guides us, guides our way. Never, ever lose your trust in God, no matter what trial He sends your way."

"Okay" Erik said, wanting to end the conversation.

'I wonder what's on his mind?' Mother wondered. 'God gives him strength to endure. And so do we. And when I hear mommies complaining: I don't know what to do to him. We walk past the store and he throws a tantrum in his face, let's go in and get lollipops. Two, not one. Because he won't leave the store without two. What a life! Everyone thinks their pain is the worst. But what is it in my child's mind and soul that he finally understands? He understood that gluten is bad for him. He understood that it was causing his tummy aches. He accepted that he wasn't allowed lollipops or anything from the corner store, the park food truck, or the store next to the kindergarten. For him, it's all a big NO. And he gets it. For his sake, maybe even for ours. Out of need or obligation. He accepts. But his mind keeps working. And he digs for truths. What a pity I can't know what he's thinking' she thought. 'I'd like to take his pain upon myself, so he'd have no further suffering. And his appetites to be painless. Because I see a deep sadness in his eyes when someone licks a lollipop noisily in the cradle next to him, or when we walk and he finds puffballs thrown on the park benches. What can I do to change his mood, to help him feel better? What's on your mind, my little child?'

"What are you thinking?" Mother dared to ask.

"Nothing" he replied, almost sighing.

"Come on, you don't have to be afraid, or ashamed... With me you know you can discuss anything. Are you sorry you can't eat like the other children?"

"Yes" he said in a lost voice.

"I understand. And I'm sorry about that, you know. It hurts my heart. But unfortunately, it's beyond my power to change the situation. You have to stay on the diet. What would make you feel better? Get you out of your funk? Shall we go buy some more gluten-free crackers?"

"Yes" he shouts, cheering up immediately!

"There you go. Now we get dressed and set up the sails! Well, why should we sit here and be upset? Come on, let's play, out with us!" concluded the mother, victorious, who immediately began to take clothes for both boys out of the wardrobe. "On the way to the park, I'll tell you about other children who are dieting" she said. "You're not the only one, you know."

"Really?" asked Erik, raising his eyebrows as he struggled to pull on a sock.

"I've told you before that there are other children in this world, and even grown-ups, who have various allergies or intolerances, whether to milk, eggs, peanuts and nuts and so on. And there are people with special diets for more serious diseases, such as diabetes. Their condition is even more delicate, because in addition to dieting, they also take medication and even injections."

"Injections?" he shouts, frightened.

"Yes. Unfortunately. That's why it's very important to follow the diet exactly and to be careful about any contamination, to prevent everything we can. Because these contaminations are dangerous. Once you eat something, it's enough to give your gut a few months of work. That's how hard it is to recover. Because there's a battle going on in the tummy, you know. With this autoimmune disease, the body considers gluten an enemy and attacks it, and in their fight, they also affect the gut. I've explained it to you before."

"Wow. Really?"

"Yeah. That's what happens with celiac disease."

"And where does celiac disease come from?"

"Like other autoimmune diseases, celiac disease is based on a genetic predisposition, but this is not enough to trigger the disease. There are various external factors that contribute to its development at any time during life. Do you understand?"

"Yes. But where are the other kids who are dieting? Do they eat the same as me?" the kid changes the subject.

"Some of them do. Others can't eat what you eat, so they eat a different, customized diet. For example, some may not eat eggs or milk. And then it's very complicated for them too, because many products contain these ingredients. That's why it's very important for everyone to read product labels very carefully. Right?"

"Yes. But I still don't know how to read. You help me,

okay?"

"Of course I do."

"Look, this is where Erik is supposed to write," he continued, pointing to the bottle of water he'd had in kindergarten during the day.

"That's right. One day you'll learn to read too. Very soon, you'll see," encouraged his mother. "But until then, it's better to concentrate on other things, not food. Because our purpose in life is not food. What do you like to do most?"

"To play."

"What would you like to play with?"

"You. Come on, shall we play?"

As Mom shakes her head in agreement, Erik shouts angrily: "You asshole!"

"Hey, what word is that? Why did you call your brother like that?"

"Well... he knocked over my cubes."

"Nothing justifies offending him or hitting him. I'm asking you nicely to behave yourself! We have all the patience in the world with you. Please behave yourself! You're a little boy, so I expect you to behave! I suppose you'll apologize to your little brother for the way you spoke to him. Even though he's still very young, he knows when you're being nice to him and when you're insulting him."

"Hm! Sorry, Dodo" said Erik with all sincerity and regret.

"I know you're an extremely valuable and sensitive little boy. I don't understand why you have such a temper issue, but together we'll work it out. I promise."

19. ERIK MAKES HIS JUSTICE

Dad leaves the room for a moment. It's now past 6 pm and everyone is tired. It's just... there's no way some people would admit that. On the contrary. They're getting excited, jumping up and down in bed and laughing loudly. Dodo does a complete imitation of Erik. He struggles to climb into bed. He clings to the edge of the cot with one hand, grabs hold of the quilt with the other and crawls with difficulty on the soft mattress. Finally, he's happy he made it. He shows his few little teeth in a funny grin, spells something out, and bounces around the bed like a little ibex. Then he follows the same route as his big brother. Up one side, down the other and having a great time. Dad watches them closely, reassured that there are times when they play so beautifully. He does, however, correct the little one when he gets out of bed.

"You still have to sit on your tummy to get down. That's it, gently, backwards. Good boy! Erik is older and more experienced. Look how his little legs hang down by the bed, almost reaching the floor," he said, to flatter him a little.

"Yes, Dodo. I'm big. You're little, you can't be like me yet. Here's what I can do. Don't worry, little one, when you grow up, you'll jump like this too" he said in a very mature tone, imitating his father, who laughed heartily and left the room for a second, thinking about how big the kid thought he was and how small he really was. He could barely get his little head up to his hip when he stood. 'Yeah... you're huge' he murmured softly to himself. But he didn't have time to finish properly when he had almost reached the kitchen door, that he had to turn back immediately from the road. Dodo was crying his eyes out, with a breath so long you'd have thought he was running out of air. Dad panicked for a moment and asked, confused:

"Did he fall? What happened?"

"No" Erik replied, smiling in the corner of his mouth.

"So? What happened to you, little man?" He insists, quickly picking him up and trying to quickly scan for any sign of a blow.

"What's all this noise?" Mom asked, coming through the bedroom door. "What's the matter, sweetie?"

No one said anything. Dad was too busy reassuring Dodo. But Mom got her maternal sense working and asked:

"Erik, did you do something to him?"

Silence. The little boy didn't dare say a word. Neither to accuse himself nor to defend himself. The mother quickly realized what had happened:

"You bit him" she said to Erik, accusing him and giving him a sad look as she examined Dodo desperately.

"Yes..." the big boy let out a slow approval through his teeth.

"How many times have I told you not to do that? How many times? I really don't know how to do this anymore... How many times have I explained you that it's not nice to do that? It's not nice to bite. Him or anyone else. It's something people don't do. Only dogs. Besides, you hurt him. You hurt him and leave marks. Have you ever put yourself in his shoes? How do you think he feels when you bite him? How would you like it if someone did that to you? Look at that!" She continued, angrily, as she pulled the baby's pants down to confirm what she had said. "Look what you've done to him! You bruised his little leg. He almost bled to tears. You want to bite a piece of him? Why are you doing that?"

"All right, let him go!" Dad interferes. "He made a mistake and I'm sure he's sorry. Besides, he won't do it again. Won't you?"

"I'm not going on about this for nothing, you know. Unfortunately, it's not his first time. He's bitten him a few times before. I've explained him it's wrong, I've teased him so many times, but he doesn't seem to understand. Well... until 2 minutes ago you were laughing and playing so nicely, and then you suddenly thought of hurting him."

"Well, Dodo doesn't let me..." he tries to defend himself.

"He won't let you what? Do what? Can you see how small he is?"

"Yes. But he won't let me get into bed. He pulls me and wants to get in first..."

"What's wrong with that? It's perfectly normal. No matter where you are, it's natural to have competition. It doesn't have to scare you. On the contrary, it should challenge you to push yourself and become even better. If you were on your own, you'd have no one to compare yourself to. Besides, there's nothing wrong with someone being ahead of you. There's room for everyone under the sun, you know..."

"What do you mean?"

"I mean the sun is up in the sky and it lights and warms the planet for everyone equally. Which is in the same place, obviously... It's up to us how we look at things. So, I suggest you be thankful you have someone to play with, practice with and even argue with. Because even sibling fights are often productive, you know. They will prepare you for encounters with other children, you will learn more easily how to manage conflicts and get into other children's game, so let's be grateful for everything we have and let's be nice to each other, shall we?"

"Uh-huh" Erik promised, nodding slightly at the same time.

In the meantime, Dad turned to face the door, holding the little boy in his arms. He seemed to have calmed down, but after the loud crying he was sleepy.

"Come on, let's go to the bathroom" Dad asked. "He is sleepy."

"Sure. But we need to establish the bite marks here" she added. "We've laid down some rules, and whoever breaks them faces the consequences. Didn't I say so?"

"Well... no."

"Yes" said the mother, decisively. "Tonight, you don't get any more cartoons and you're not allowed in Dodo's bed."

"Why, Mommy?"

"Because that's the punishment for biting. And tomorrow you and I are gonna talk about it again!"

20. ERIK WANTS HIS MOTHER'S ATTENTION

How could a mother's heart divide into two, three, or however many it would take for her and her babies? Because no school in the world teaches you that, and it would have been so useful to know such a thing... 'Oh, my time hasn't belonged to me for so long. And yet, if I give it all to them, I'd like to know they're happy. But it's not working for me,' thought Mom.

"Oh, and this squash is so hard to peel" she finally said aloud, leaning over to Dodo, who had his little finger in his mouth, and with his other hand he had grabbed hold of her leg and was twirling around it, grunting.

"God, you're tired. I have to give you your snack too, I don't know how time flies" she said, wiping her hands and bending down to his level. At that moment, her emotions overwhelmed her even more:

'What am I doing wrong? Can't I organize myself in such a way that I can take better care of you? I miss holding you in my arms more!' she said, picking him up and hugging him tightly to her chest. 'I'm burning with longing to comfort you and play with you... I feel overwhelmed by everything and my heart is bubbling over in a sea of sadness. I don't want you to grow up around me. I want you to grow up with me. To look at you more than at the pots of food, the laundry waiting to be ironed, or the toys strewn around the house. When did things get so out of control?' she thought to herself, tears streaming down her face as Dodo noisily sucked his little finger.

"Okay, fine. I don't think you feel like eating anything but milk right now. Here's another missed meal. Come on, let's get you ready for sleep. At least let's enjoy this private moment together."

The little one was certainly enjoying himself, as he hungrily swallowed the milk while he struggled to get his little socks out of his little feet.

"What a habit you have" she said. "You can't eat unless you're barefoot" she remarked, and a smile suddenly brightened her face. But only for a second. Because the thought ran back to Erik. She couldn't remember him having any of that kind of snuggle when he was breastfeeding. But she liked to hold his breast a lot, play some more, go away and come back. For Dodo, on the other hand, there was no time for that. Besides, it also shortened his time for sucking for fear of Erik getting even more jealous of him because he spent so much time in mommy's arms. So, somewhat forced by circumstances, the kid got used to eating quickly and then going about his business elsewhere.

"Little baby" she said. "I rushed you with the milk... You get bread and other gluten products from Thursday to Easter, for fear of giving Erik an appetite... I feel so guilty about that. I don't want to deprive you of anything. And yet I have to do what's best for both of you." And again, she falls into that state of frustration, of emotions running high, of overwhelm. She left the satiated baby in the crib, gave him a corner of a fluffy blanket to sleep peacefully, and went back to her business. Tears streaming down her cheeks, like the child she had left at nursery this morning. She couldn't get his sad little face out of her mind, with red eyes and snot hanging almost in his mouth from crying. He begged her to take him home, he clung with all his strength to the pram, he resisted in every way, and yet she left him there. She left... but her heart remained in the kindergarten alley, crumbled to pieces. And all day long she thought of him. The way he begged her. The way he cried 'I don't want to stay here. I want to go home with you. I want to stay with YOU.' And she let him... She let him. What was in his heart then? Such disappointment. Such sadness... pain... maybe even anger. The one he loved most left him. She didn't care about anything. She left without listening to his desperate prayers. 'What a deep wound of abandonment have I inflicted on my child?' she wondered, sobbing. 'How long will we work to repair this trauma? I know I'm not doing him any good' she thought. 'And yet there was no choice. The rules clearly state that for several unexcused absences, he can lose his place in kindergarten. And then there's no money to go to a private kindergarten. If only I could at least get into the classroom with him, possibly sit there with him for an hour or two, until he settles in... What a bad time we live in. The pandemic has taken so much from us...' The ringing of the phone takes her by surprise, frightens her.

"Were there any other kids crying at the door, or what was going on, I mean, like today?" asked the father, curious.

"There was only one other child, an older one, crying. The others came, said goodbye to their parents and quietly entered the building."

"Didn't we talk last night about how nice it is in kindergarten, that they play, do activities, that the ladies are nice and so on?"

"Well, yes. And he really does walk there very cheerfully. We enter the courtyard, and as soon as we reach the front of the building, he doesn't want to get out of the pram. Suddenly he changes his mind and says: 'I want to go home with you. I don't want to stay.' And from there, a whole circus that tears my soul apart. He doesn't want to get out of the pram, instead Dodo jumps on his back, I barely manage to hold him. I told you the other day I didn't know what to do and I left him on the floor in his socks. He saw a windmill and started to spell: 'mom, look, mom...' walking towards the windmill. I was trying to convince Erik to get out of the stroller, and when I almost succeeded, I saw Dodo walking away towards another windmill, towards the gate of the unit, among the parents rushing their children. I leave Erik for two seconds and run to retrieve the little one. I put him next to the cart and try to hold him with my feet, to resume negotiations with Erik, who had settled back comfortably on the cart and had fastened his seatbelts this time. Large beads of sweat rolled down my back. The ladies at the entrance see me out of my depth and offer to help. They pick him up too, but the boy doesn't react to anyone or anything. I promise I'll come and get him first, tell him I love him, give him a hug, promise him his favourite biscuits, games in the afternoon and the moon and stars. I have the impression that at those moments he doesn't see me, he doesn't hear me. He's just going on and on about 'I want to stay with you'. And when the nurse finally took him in her arms, because I didn't know what to do to him, he shouted: 'Just come out of the kitchen and come? Will you just come out of the kitchen, Mommy? Yes, Mommy?' It breaks my heart in those moments. I really don't know how to react."

"I believe you. It's a delicate situation. We'll try talking to him at home again, see what happens. Maybe there's something he doesn't like there. Besides the food, I mean. Anyway, keeping him at home isn't a solution either. You get him out of his routine and he reacts even worse. If you kept him at home with you yesterday, he would cry even more today, because it was setting a precedent. We have to be very careful with that. He'll settle in, slowly."

"I agree. But I find this accommodation so brutal. He's only three. What are we talking about? And he's my kid. It hurts me to leave him there every day crying" she said, bursting into tears again.

"Come on! Calm down! It'll be all right! We have strong boys and they'll adapt easily."

"See? That's just it. He keeps thinking Dodo's coming home with me. He's the only one getting off the wagon. Only he stays there. And he asks me why I don't leave the little one. How can I assure him of my love?"

"Calm down. I'm just saying you're a little more vulnerable now. We're having a harder time and you're overwhelmed with housework, projects. Plus, you're on 24-hour a day with the baby, you wake up a lot at night, the fatigue has built up. Come on, take it easy and you'll see things will be fine. I told you he also cries when I leave him in the morning. So even when I'm alone and we don't have the pram with us. You know he did the same thing when I took him to nursery. He had a hard time adjusting, but in the end he was fine. Promise that after I hang up the phone, you'll wash your face and send me a picture of you smiling?" Dad managed to get a smile out of her already. Her face brightened a little, and she could see the day ahead with more hope.

'Let's focus then' she said to herself. And she quickly made her plan: 'We'll put on some music, check the kindergarten menu for tomorrow, and while I'm preparing the ingredients I might as well sort out the laundry to put in the wash. Then, while the food is on the stove, I'll collect the laundry that's already dry. For the ironing... I don't know when it will be the clothes' turn. I also have to pick up the toys Dodo spread around, to feed him when he wakes up, then we'll get ready to go after Erik. I'll keep them out in the fresh air for a bit, and tonight when Daddy comes, I'll make a plan for the cleaning while he keeps them busy, and the work... Fortunately it's a long night and I have some quiet time to write. That way I'll get some energy...'

She'd read a lot about postpartum depression. But, like everyone else, she thought it couldn't happen to her.

Unfortunately, she realized that she was suffering from the problem. She felt helpless, guilty, overwhelmed and sometimes had ugly, conflicting thoughts that scared her. She was so tired, that she began to wonder what others would do without her if anything happened to her. What would become of her children if she was gone? Who would take care of them afterwards? Why wouldn't that person come and help her now? She didn't like having all kinds of things like that running through her mind, but she really couldn't control herself. It was beyond her control. She'd tried a few times to tell her husband that she wasn't feeling well, that she was just overwhelmed, but he blamed it all on fatigue, every time.

'Oh... sometimes I wish I could go back to the regular job, with a schedule' she said to herself one day. 'Just for the sake of talking quietly with other adults without someone pulling my leg.' But it wasn't seconds after that thought that her mind was invaded by other questions: 'what am I going to do when these two little guys get sick? Or how am I going to keep everything under control at home when I can barely manage to cook for kindergarten, take care of the house and the kids now? How am I going to proceed when I get home at 6-7 pm, tired after a day's work, and then get on with everything there is to do. I'm certainly not the first in this situation, nor the last. The other moms in the park have been through the same thing, and now they are calm and seem at peace with the situation. Except... they only have one child, and those who have two, have a grandmother, aunt, nanny to help. Anyway. Faith and patience. I don't think God gives us more than we can handle' she tries to encourage herself, and returns to the kitchen to clean carrots and celery. She had to move fast, while the toddler was still asleep. The laundry was in the washing machine and the toys were now waiting meekly in their boxes, to be discovered and "awakened" to life again when the baby woke up.

21. I'M NOT THE ONLY MARTIAN

Erik reveals that there is another boy at kindergarten who eats differently from his classmates, just like him. He feels more comfortable now that his classmates' curious eyes are no longer just on him at mealtimes. His mother suggests that he ignore the others and mind his own business.

"It doesn't matter what others eat or what they think, you know? All you care about is being well. That's all. There'll always be one or two people to comment. That's life. If they don't have something to say, people don't feel good. And when they can tease someone, they seem even happier."

"What is teasing?"

"Well... to annoy, in other words. To hurt them."

"Well, why would they want that?"

"I don't know. That's how the Bad Guy gets his tail."

"Who's the bad guy?"

"Well... every little child has a guardian angel who looks after him. There are other angels, bad angels, who come and make children do bad things, you know? More or less like this. The important thing is to listen to the good angel. We should ask ourselves if our behaviour is not upsetting those around us, if we are not hurting them, and we should always act according to the answer of this question."

"Good."

"Would you like to meet other children in your situation who are on a diet?" asked Mom. She had tried to have this conversation with him before.

"Yes..." said the child, feeling insecure. The mother quickly realised that he didn't know exactly what that meant, had no idea where his mind was going. 'On the one hand it's a good thing' she thought to herself. 'It confirms what doctors say, that on the one hand it's easy to work with children in the sense that their eating habits, lifestyles and so on are now being formed. But on the other hand, no doctor has told her how to deal with the situation from a psychological point of view, and especially with the food gap between such young siblings. What a complicated job' she thought. Not even the psychologist who works with children gave her any hope that she could help more than the family...

"Mommy..." Erik said, interrupting the movie script running in her mind.

"Yes. Sorry... I've been thinking a bit, baby. Well, I'll do my best to put you in touch with other gluten-intolerant kids, try to find some common activities and, who knows, maybe you'll make some nice friends in the future. Sounds good?"

"Yes. I want to have lots of friends."

"Sure, sure," she said in a deep voice, laughing. "And you'll share the toys too, right?"

"Eh... we'll see about that," the little boy replied half-mouthed, shaking his shoulders.

"You'll see you're not a Martian. You're just like all the other kids, only your body needs to eat a little differently."

"Mar what? Could you repeat that, please?"

"Mar-tian. It means someone different from us humans who doesn't live on planet Earth, but on Mars."

"You mean..."

"I mean, we're gonna read the book again about the sun, moon, stars... remember? That's where we read about the planets. You're still little, but I'll tell you more if you want."

"Yes. If I want to. But right now, I'd like something to eat. Anyway. Do you have anything for me? What can I eat?"

"Of course, I have something for you. I'll tell you what we've got, and you choose!"

"You pick!"

"Well, I'm not going to! I'm sorry. I've chosen what to put in the fridge, from there you tell me what you want, from what I show you. You have to make your own choices. Like when you ask for cookies, okay?"

"Well, I want biscuits! I do!"

"That's not what this is about. I've already explained to you that you only get biscuits at snack time."

"Well, isn't this the snack?"

"You're such a smart-ass! No. At the first snack, at 10

o'clock, you get fruit, we follow the kindergarten schedule exactly, and at the afternoon snack you get cake or biscuits, yoghurt, generally something sweet."

"Well, what time is it now? Can't I get it now?"

"Now it's evening and you'll get dinner. Snack tomorrow. At the appointed time."

"But, Mommy..."

"I know, darling... I don't like to refuse you, but you must understand there are certain rules we must follow. It's three meals a day and two snacks. Fruit in the first part of the day and sweets preferably as few as possible and eaten as a snack. If it were up to you, you would ask for and eat biscuits all day. And it's not healthy to do so. Especially since a lot of grains are already excluded from your menu, it's very important to eat more balanced, or just barely."

"Okay, Mommy."

"Come on, don't be sad. It hurts me to see you like this. We'll go to the bathroom after lunch and I'll tell you a story, okay?"

"The one with Eric!"

"Okay, okay, okay."

"You're starting now?"

"Now we chew, focus on food, and at bedtime I'll tell you the story. As promised."

The meal is going pretty quietly. When hungry, the child eats alone, swallows quickly and hungrily like a hungry wolf. Then, when the tummy is just about full, he puts the spoon down and begins to recline in the big dining chair.

"Will you help me? Please!"

Dad laughed heartily, but didn't intervene.

"So far you've done very well," said Mom. "Come on, you can do it! You've got very little left. That is, if you're still hungry..."

"I am."

"So what? What's the matter?"

"I want you to give it to me! Please!"

"Come on, you feed him and I'll feed Dodo," said Dad. "That's why he acts like that, you know! There's no need to stand firm now and create conflict. He's tired and he can start from anything."

Mother resigned herself and began spoon-feeding Erik like a little boy. He stood there gaping like a hungry baby turkey. Lying on his back and tired, he was leaking out of his dining chair.

"Ma-ma," he suddenly hissed, desperately trying to get up from the stool as quickly as possible. His eyes twinkled with excitement and he seemed to tremble with anticipation.

"Come on, sit down, please!" intervened Dad again. "You don't have to pretend to be Dodo. He's younger and you mustn't do like him, please! I insist."

Erik had stood up because he had seen Dodo do this, and his request to be fed came also through the power of imitation. He'd been acting like this for a while, trying to get the attention of his parents, desperate for his behavior. 'There's no end to this regression,' thought Mom. 'He's keeping it up for almost a year. I can't wait for him to get back on track, to see him evolve and be an example to this little one, not the other way around.' Instead, the youngest is learning a lot by watching his older brother, and learning to play, climb and do various activities by skipping steps, which the other had discovered in his own time slowly, step by step, on his own. He was now watching and imitating, astonishing his parents every day with his rapid progress. It was a rewarding thing, on the one hand, though it's also nice to explore, to discover on his own. Erik, on the other hand, was doing his best to act like a baby. 'It reminds me of that story about the dog and the donkey,' she thought. When the beast of burden was envious of the puppy because, although he didn't do any work, he got all day long attention and caresses, he was pampered and loved, and he sat alone in the stable. So, he studied the dog's behaviour for days and decided to do as he did, and one day when the owner came home, the donkey jumped on his back, just as the dog did, scaring the poor man to death. The moral was: everyone must behave as he is, and he will be appreciated and loved for what he is. If he didn't caress him all day like the dog, it didn't mean the man didn't appreciate the donkey equally. Although... that wasn't the case here, because parents do their best to give both of them more or less equal time. On the contrary, the little one is often left out, the focusing attention is mostly on the big one.

"Come on, give us the bread!" the father asked her once again, in a heavy tone! "Why are you so thoughtful?"

"God's ways are twisted," said the woman in a low voice, more as if to herself. Then she went on: "It's hard with these emotions. Managing them is an art, which unfortunately we don't master yet. I hope we do our best for them."

"Yes, the food is very good. I like it" Erik said.

Mom and Dad laughed uproariously. And they watched with admiration and love as he chewed gently, delicately, savoring every bite. After all, what is happiness? A moment, a feeling when you realize how fulfilled, content and at peace you are with what you have, the moment when you realize that simply existing is a blessing. And you try to engrave that moment in your mind, to access the memory when you hit hard times, to have a place from where to draw strength, inspiration, the will to go on and live beautifully.

22. BETWEEN DESIRES, DIET AND RESPONSIBILITY

*

Celiac disease is a challenge not only for the patient but also for the family. When the sufferer is a child, things get more complicated, because many of the advice given by the doctors themselves are difficult to apply, the mental state is difficult to manage. As a parent, you actually get stuck when you hear them ask, in a sad and lost voice: 'But what about gluten, when am I allowed to eat? I want to eat like everyone else, anything.' In those moments, the mind would like to find something rational, anything, to justify his refusal, but basically it remains the same, a refusal, and his ears can't process beyond "no", whatever you tell him. You can tell by the blank, lost look in his eyes, the lost voice, the posture he takes in those moments, when you, as an adult, want to go into the ground with nerves and helplessness, bite down on a clenched fist and it still wouldn't hurt, how hard his pain is... There's a lot of pain there, as much as we'd like to make it all seem nice for him. And, beyond that, parents need to step back, step back, rebuild their voice and take a stand. There's another child out there who depends on them.

Because where there is another child in the family with a celiac child, with a normal diet, the challenge is much bigger. And I think every parent in this situation is curious to know... how others have managed their situation? What did they do? How did they handle it? So, he can validate what he's doing, or not doing good. To take a better example or simply to see that they are not alone in their situation. Just as they are trying to help Erik, explaining that there are others like him, so parents need support, encouragement... Because there are times when they, too, feel overwhelmed and need a shoulder to cry on.

Seen from the outside, the situation may seem simple: 'The appropriate behaviour would be to give up gluten completely in the kitchen where the celiac patient lives, to keep them out of trouble,' the doctor recommends. But the question is: is it nutritionally correct to deprive the other child in the house of gluten? Of course not. And so, say the doctors, who recommend eating gluten until the child is tested at around one and a half year old. So how would it be more appropriate to proceed? Erik's parents have seen fit to go 90-95% gluten-free, in the sense that they don't cook anything with gluten at home for themselves and their big boy. All pots and pans and kitchen utensils have been replaced with new, uncontaminated ones, except for a cooking pot, bowl and cutlery, inscribed with Dodo's name, which are washed with a separate dish sponge, and afterwards Mom takes care to clean the sink as best she can. For the younger boy, the parents have set up a special drawer where they keep a few biscuits and some cereal that can be made with milk, usually when his big brother is not at home. Otherwise, the baby gets a corner of a bagel or a pastry outside the house. So far, things seem clear, and settled. The children are small and manage the situation as easily as possible. Despite mom's frustration at not cooking the little one any pancakes, not showing him the taste of freshly baked cake, sugar-sprinkled doughnuts and... hot bread.

But what happens when you go outside? Slowly, acquaintances have begun to learn that Erik is not allowed to eat gluten, and don't offer him anything but fruit, eventually. But can Dodo get anything else from people around him? The shock will be huge for Erik at that moment... What a nasty situation it was when, one day on the way to kindergarten, mom bought Dodo a bagel. Most of it fell on the floor, and the little piece that remained in his hand, he turned it over on all sides, sucked it, and molted it as best he could, grunting with pleasure. Mother was fond of him, seeing how eagerly he was grinding the gluten bomb, so she felt sorry to snatch it out of his hand before he stepped through the kindergarten entrance gate. The first thing Erik asked, after making sure Mom brought his favorite snack, was: "What is he eating?" No more Dodo, baby or otherwise. It was with jealousy, with envy... Mom gave him the gluten-free breadsticks, a big bag, and said: "Look what I brought you, a big bag of breadsticks, your favorite." The little boy couldn't see or hear. He no longer rushed at the snack, as before, but approached the stroller slowly, holding out his hand suddenly. Mother was taken by surprise, but still had time to react. She grabbed his hand, lowered herself to his level, looked him in the eye and said:

"I'm sorry. They' re with gluten. Please take the breadsticks! These will do you good." But the child was not satisfied. He pushed himself up her side and kept staring at the spit-soaked bagel, on which a few sesame seeds were still visible.

"May I put my hand on it?" he said, almost begging...

"Sorry, baby. I'd rather you didn't. The gluten stays on your hand and I won't be able to wash you until we get home, and you'll want to eat your breadsticks! Please, please, please!"

The child looked down and turned away. He was holding back tears. 'What's in his heart?' the mother wondered. 'What's the damn gluten burden? But how will the poor people who are diabetic, for example, who have to take treatments on top of their diet, manage? God forbids! Oh, great God, give us the strength to carry them all, You know best what You are doing!' They all walked slowly home. Mother pushed the stroller, and Erik walked beside her, quietly chewing.

"What did you do at the kindergarten today?"

"It was fine."

"Who did you play with?"

"The kids."

"Were there many of you today?"

"Yes, there were."

"And what activities did you do there?"

"Eh... activities. We colored with our fingers."

"And what did the ladies say? Did they teach you any poems today?"

"Uh..."

'God, he's locking inside him... I don't like this at all,' thought Mom. 'What can I do to bring him closer to me?'

But, unfortunately, the way things were going wasn't helping.

"Wait, I want to hold his hand!"

"Let him go! Just sit there. Give me your hand."

"No, no, no, no, no, no. I want to take him."

"Come on, please!" She insists in a gentle voice.

By this time, as the boy was leaning in front of the trolley, Dodo was getting active and trying to be friendly with him, holding out his wrinkled gluten bagel hands. Erik also reached out, but Mom intervened just in time, just before the two of them touched hands.

"Come on, you guys go on playing in the house, please, after we've washed our hands thoroughly!"

"But look how cute he is, Erik said... he wants to shake hands with me, to caress me. What do you want to do, you little one?'" he said, pushing himself better in front of the wagon and unclasping his hand from his mother's. Dodo kept squirming and stretching his hand, in which he was holding the bagel, towards the other man's mouth, whispering: "eh, eh..." and gesturing like someone who actually wants to stuff something in your mouth. Mom grabs Erik from the front of the cart, taking him in her arms! She couldn't think of another way to get his mouth away from the temptation that was pushing itself towards him. The boy burst into tears, screaming as loud as he could:

"Let me down, let me down!" and the mother tried to calm him, pretending to reproach the little boy:

"Didn't I tell you his tummy hurts if you give him that? We have to take care of him too and give him only what is good for him. Be resonable, will you, Dodo?" Hearing this, Erik calmed down. He wiped his tears with his sleeve, cried deeply and said:

"I just wanted a taste! When I have something, I give it to him too!"

"I know, baby!" said the mother, deeply affected by the little boy's words. She had taught them to share everything they had, and the little one did nothing wrong. The only one who had done wrong was her, who should have snatched the gluten crap out of his hand and disinfected his hands before he reached the kindergarden. She would have then avoided this whole scene that caused conflict between the brothers. 'God, if only that was all' she thought to herself. 'How many times will there be when the little one will eat gluten products and Erik will just watch? What a tragedy.' She felt her heart breaking, shattered into a thousand pieces. 'How will he feel when we are somewhere, anywhere, and someone offers them something with gluten, we'll say <thanks, he's not allowed, but you can give it to Dodo, he can eat anything>' she was happy for the little one, but she was in pain about what was happening to the big one.

'Why does God do such injustice?' she thought. 'Why, if he is so great and good, would he allow children to suffer? Why are there children with cancer, with diabetes, with these horrible allergies? Why does my child have to go through this? My child...' She knew everything was for a reason, that God doesn't give more than one can bear, and that He knows best what He's doing... but it seemed like sometimes it was too much. She wanted to be able to do less. To close her eyes and wake up to a reality where everything is nice, without restrictions and meanness. Unfortunately, that wasn't possible at the moment, and she knew she had to be strong. For them, for the children.

    **

'I am in control of my children's lives. In quotes. In the sense that I can control them, I can direct what and how they eat. At least now, while they're young. What do we do with the others instead? she kept thinking. She remembered a birthday party they'd had at home shortly after his diagnosis. They'd had a few guests and had made serious preparations, with appetizers, steak, salads and cake. All gluten-free. Appetizing and delightful. After the appetizer was served, one of the guests said: "The bread is missing!" Used to large baskets of bread on the table, in abundance, for crumbs to spill out and for everyone to feast on, now he hadn't even noticed the basket of gluten-free bread sitting discreetly in the centre of the table. "It's on the table," his wife whispered, gesturing discreetly. The guest realised his mistake and was embarrassed, and the family was already uncomfortable with the whole scene. At the time they didn't know how to address the issue and simply avoided it, avoiding the subject in front of the child. Later, as the parents kept talking to Erik and explaining the situation, they began to sit down with regular eaters when the situation required it. Parents try to educate the child and help him to realise the importance of diet, but others also need to be made aware when their behaviour can put him at risk, even unintentionally. Because contamination lurks at every turn and is found even in the most unsuspected things. And a simple loaf of bread brought into the house can put the celiac at risk. How does this happen?

For example, even if guests eat bread in the kitchen in the absence of the celiac, and clean the tableside thoroughly, they need to pay attention to all the details: where the bread was cut, preferably not on the wood chopping board, after they've got their hands on the bread what else have they done? Maybe they touched the salt in the salt shaker with their gluten fingers, then this is also used for the preparation of celiac food... As for gluten foods, if they still exist in the house, they should not be kept on top of the kitchen stove or on a top shelf, so that particles do not fall on gluten-free products. These are small details, tiny little things that can make the difference between good and bad. Because every particle of gluten swallowed brings the celiac one step closer to the unpleasantness and symptoms. This is why parents have chosen to stop consuming gluten at home and are constantly informing themselves, enrolling in courses on the subject and also taking up the subject of nutrition. And they try to follow the rules not only at home but also on their travels, where things are even harder to control.

23. "WHEN WILL I BE ALLOWED TO EAT GLUTEN?"

"Why can't people understand that celiac disease is a disease with no cure in the present?" was another question that gave her no peace. Isn't it enough she has to explain to her child, almost daily, that he' s not allowed gluten, why and for how long? The last question he asked her bothered her the most.

"When can I eat gluten? Will I never be allowed to eat gluten?" Erik asked her, in his sad voice, in a moment of silence and meditation. Mom began to hate the subject, because she didn't know what else to say to him. It wasn't enough for him to speak, to tell the truth, he wanted her to say something to make him feel better. Because the truth was cruel for a child of only three. How do you start out in life with hope when you're met with rejection?

"But I want to consume, Mommy. I want lactose and gluten, like the other children!" he said in a cat-like voice, as if mercy had come from his mother, not nature.

'How can I explain it to him?" she wondered. How to approach the matter so that he understands it is not I personally who refuse him, but that it is beyond my power. She felt her soul wasted and wished she could make herself small, that she could be a child and he an adult, that she could no longer carry so great a responsibility on her shoulders. In addition to managing the relationship with the child, she also had to waste energy with those around her, to convince them of the seriousness of the situation. Her own mother, Erik's grandmother, insisted that maybe it wasn't so bad if he had a taste, and her mother was afraid that such remarks might make her child hopeful and, worse, somehow curious. Sometimes she seemed to understand how serious it was. At other times, out of a desire to get rid of this burden, which seemed very heavy to her, she would bring up all sorts of things, which made the pain even worse, such as: he should consult other specialists, maybe the diagnosis is wrong, maybe when he is 6-7 years old he will be able to eat normally and so on... 'How sad that the family itself makes things so difficult, when there are so many other details to be taken care of' she thought.

For example, at the last doctor's visit, she received a food diary to be filled in for 3 days, so the menu will be correlated with the test results. Is the child eating well enough? That was another of her fears. And she had often thought of consulting a specialist on the matter. But the first one she had managed to get in touch with hadn't convinced her that he really knew what was going on. She cooks her daily menu at home for the kindergarten, but would like to know if simply replacing normal bread and pasta with similar gluten-free products would still preserve the nutritional balance. Because the lack of such an important food group as grains, which are at the base of the food pyramid, seemed very important to her. In addition, the child refuses nuts, seeds and raw vegetables from the start, which was another minus. 'What should one do? If only the day had more than 24 hours, so she could study everything in depth, quickly...' thought. She smiled and sighed, then returned to her conversation with the child. But what... what would such a small child understand?

24. ERIK ALONE WITH GRANDPARENTS

Just like Little Red Riding Hood, who prepares her basket of supplies to visit grandma, Erik packs his favourite monkey, picks out a few toys and a few changes of clothes and prepares to go on holiday to grandma and grandpa. He's happy to change the surroundings. He plans to go for walks, play all day, and never get nagged about not picking up his toys. Grandma has already promised him that she'll do everything he wants, but that's exactly what Mom is afraid of, that he won't be pampered too much... he wants Dodo to go with him, but his grandparents explain that he's still too babyish. So, he says goodbye to his little brother, who looks at him puzzled, rubbing his sleepy eyes, and comforts him:

"Forget it, you'll grow up a bit and you'll go to grandma, don't be sad. I'll call you every day and we'll talk on video. Okay, little one?" Mom and grandparents smile when they see him talking just like a big man and laugh when Erik pats Dodo on the head in consolation. But Dodo didn't quite realize what was going on, and it was only when they were all out the door that he recovered and started waving shyly, sending them kisses and saying "bye-bye" over and over again. The grandparents quickly went downstairs with Erik, before he changed his mind and came back to ask for Mommy and Dodo. He would go anywhere with Grandma and Grandpa, but he misses Mom too...

With grandparents, time seems to stand still. Here, everything is transposed into another dimension. The child plays for hours with his grandmother, then asks her to make him rice pudding, doughnuts and whatever else he fancies. He sits outside for half a day when it's warm, he wanders around the chickens, feeds the dog, which he's still a bit afraid of, collects plums, spreads sand in the yard, waters the pavement, runs his bike and he is happy. Sometimes he misses his mother, and wants to call her on the video, but his grandmother has explained that they can't talk on the phone all the time, and especially in the evening, when he misses her and tries to distract him in the best way, they know...

Grandpa plays the horse and rides him on the tractor, Grandma plays all his games and does all his cravings, and when he goes to his other grandma, she catches his pigtails and teaches him to sew. They put up pickles together, plant flowers and prepare food for lunch. The child is happy to stay outside a lot, runs around freely and plays nicely with the children in the narrow alley. He misses his little brother, but time passes quickly and he enjoys every moment in the yard. The neighbours' little girl keeps him company and they play together every day. Everything is wonderful until the moment they have to share something. His parents and grandparents have always explained to him that it's nice to give what you have to others, especially since you want to receive from others. And if others don't see you doing this, and thus becoming an example for them, they will adopt the same behaviour and not share either.

"No, that' s mine" Erik said.

"Give it to me! I want it, too," cried the little girl angrily.

"Give her the bike," said the grandmother.

"No. It's mine. I don't want it" the little boy said.

"But we've been over this. Look, she'll give you her toy too. Come on, exchange a little, because that's nice" said Grandma, in a gentle voice.

"Yes, but... No" he shouted loudly again, after he seemed to have softened a little.

Grandma didn't insist. She took the little girl aside and apologized on his behalf:

"I'm sorry. Well, it's his, and now he's not willing to share it. Come and play with something else now! Don't be sad!"

"No. I want it too. Now!" she said upset. "I want it a little!"

"Hey! How am I supposed to get you two back together?"

"Come on, my lovely Erik, give her the bike. Just one ride. Look, while you're riding her baby doll."

"No" he said. "She didn't give me cookies either. Why should I share?"

Grandma blushed and shivered uncontrollably. She was in trouble, and she was sorry now she had insisted.

"Yeah, I know what you mean. But you weren't allowed to eat any of those biscuits anyway. You know what I mean?"

"Yeah, I know what you mean. I know what you mean. That they're made with gluten" he said, decisively.

"Well, so what, grandma? Why are you reacting like this? You know those biscuits would have made you sick. That's why she didn't give them to you. To protect you."

"Yeah. But I want to have something for myself, too. Something I won't give to them."

Grandma's eyes watered. She felt so sorry for him. She would have done anything to keep the little boy from going through this. She felt like she was witnessing a battle. In a camp he was fighting. He alone. And on the other side was the rest of the world. A whole world that could share things. And only he didn't have something of his own. That's when she got the idea to join this fight with him, not to leave him alone, to make him feel better. What doesn't grandparents think of, for grandchildren's sakes?

"Ah. I see what this is about now. Good. I won't insist. Sorry. Look, you can keep the bike to yourself, okay? Don't give it to anyone. And I won't get mad. But one thing I want you to understand, please: if someone doesn't give you gluten crackers, it's not out of malice, it's because we asked them to, to protect you. Do you understand? We just want you to be well. That's all. Here's my idea. Do you want to try to make some cookies or biscuits together, or whatever? And they'll be just for you. What do you say?"

"Yes" shouts the boy, happy. "I do. Shall we do it now?"

"We will," said grandma. "And so, it was time to retire. We've stayed long enough at the children. Let's say goodbye. Say goodbye to Alexis and let's follow up on our little secret."

"Bye, Alexis," said the boy. "Next time, maybe... Maybe I'll give you the bike" he blurted out, slowly, but not quite convinced of what he'd said.

"Good boy. That's my boy," said Grandma. "Come on, let's get to work, now!"

Once in the backyard, they washed their hands thoroughly and went into the kitchen to prepare the ingredients for something sweet and tasty...

Grandma put out the package of gluten-free flour. It was a flour from a grain mix she'd never even heard of until recently. She pulled a small bowl out of the cupboard and began measuring out the ingredients. She shrugged and sighed, thinking about how they used to make doughnuts and bagels before diagnosis. When the baby was full of flour from head to toe, he would grind his tiny hands and make patties, laughing heartily. Now he was a little older, a little more serious, sometimes even more mature, and Grandma felt that the disease was robbing him of his childhood innocence. It had forced him to be responsible too soon.

"Let's see how much flour we need. We'll measure it together and then you will pour the milk, we'll break the eggs and after mixing together we'll make the shapes. Are you ready?" The little boy nods his head and the two set to work with great enthusiasm. After all, happiness lies in simple things, it's a wonderful feeling that comes from accepting restrictions and welcoming all the other little things in life that we often don't see, don't realize.

25 AVOIDING RESTAURANTS

Erik is excited about the mountain trip. He grabs his mother's hand tightly and pulls her up quickly:

"Come on, let's go up there!"

"Right away," she tells him. "We set up the trolley and then we go. Anyway, it's foggy all over the region and we can't see much. There's no need to hurry now. Let's enjoy the fresh mountain air."

"All right, but come on! What's that smell?"

Mom puts her head down, pretending she still has to put things on the stroller and settle the baby.

"What's that smell?" Erik insists, this time turning to Grandma.

"It's food, babe," Mom finally replies. "It smells like restaurant food."

"I want to go to the restaurant!" he shouts. "Come on, let's go!"

Parents and grandparents look at each other. It was one of those moments when they were not sure what to do, but no one dared to shake the child's burning desire. What had he done wrong, the little boy, to be told no all the time? Then, grandma had an idea:

"We could... we could go for a cup of tea, if you like."

"Yes. I want tea with biscuits! And some meat!", Erik filled in after everyone's face had brightened, as if the problem had been solved.

"Well, no meat," Grandma explained. "Do you know how beautiful it is up here in the mountains? We can watch the sheep, go look at horses, look for ducks, maybe even find a swing if we walk a little. You like swinging, don't you?"

The child's attention had been distracted from the restaurant and the delicious smell of food. Once again, Grandma demonstrated her pacifying abilities. Then, so as not to leave him thinking about the food he hadn't received, she took him aside and asked:

"Would you fancy a nice cheese and ham sandwich? Or would you like some fruit? I've got a surprise for you in your green dinosaur backpack. And after the walk we'll go to our accommodation and have a great barbecue with salad. You'll help us, right?"

Enthusiastically, Erik accepts the sandwich and the apple a little later... he would have eaten even the dinosaur on the backpack. And his parents were overjoyed that the fresh mountain air gave him such an appetite.

"Hey, you're right, there's some sheep down there... Can we go to them?"

Mom nods approval, grabs his hand and they set off together towards the group of sheep. The two of them have fun, walking on the path and the wet grass. They reach muddy stretches and get mud on their shoes, but nothing else matters. The objective is the sheeps and getting to them. When they get close, however, the dogs make their presence felt. First three, then four, and the mother is no longer walking as confidently as she started out.

"I think it would be prudent to stop, darling!"

"But they're so close... Let's go to them, please! Can I ride one?"

"Of course not," laughed Mother. "Sheep aren't horses."

"But why not? Why can't I get on?"

"Because every animal has its own purpose. Just as cows give milk, sheeps also give milk and wool. Their fur can be used to make clothes, blankets, all sorts of things. The horse, on the other hand, is a draught animal, like the donkey. You can climb on it. Although, for your height, I think a pony would be more appropriate."

"But, Mommy, I'm big. And I can. Remember when we went riding, and we rode a giant horse? I did very well. When are we going again? Come on, let's go closer to the sheeps!" he added quickly, before Mom could answer his question.

'How beautiful it is in the middle of the nature,' the woman thought. 'Here ends the story of a sad, restricted child, who cannot enjoy at leisure everything around him, as if his senses should be locked away somewhere, where he can't ask questions that can only be answered in the negatives. Here he is, at last, away from shops and temptations. How wonderful! He's so happy. And his happiness is touching us all. It fills our souls and brings us a state of peace, of contentment. We are so small in such a big world, and souls seem daily like care-laden stones. We rarely have, or rather rarely allow ourselves to take a moment to quiet our minds and souls. The daily schedule is so tight, so many tasks are squeezed into the agenda, that we forget even to breathe. And that's not a metaphor. People actually forget to breathe deeply, abdominal, breathe short, fast, as if they were running away... My children would like to learn to enjoy life, any little moment or thing to connect a smile, a hope. To thank the Universe every day for what they get, for what they have, and to always keep their arms wide open to welcome what is to come. Many pray, ask for things from the divine, but do not open their arms to receive them. Child, be confident that if you desire something with all your being, it will come. Never stop hoping! Faith moves mountains. Whatever you believe, it can be done.' Mother gets a lump in her throat, and wakes up whispering aloud: 'What a revelation!' Then she thinks of the years she prayed to God to give her a child, or as many as He wants, of her desperate prayers, of the countless visits to doctors who told her they had no explanation for what was happening to her, because the tests were perfectly normal. She also thinks of her mother, how hard she fought to beat cancer, how hard she prayed and believed. Yes. This is it. If you believe something, but with your whole being, nothing can stop you. And then his father's words come to mind, 'Who knows, maybe in a few years some vaccine will come along and he can be cured!' Mom knows, as does Dad, that celiac disease is an autoimmune disease. And that unfortunately there is no cure yet. She approves of it, but deep down she tries to get used to the idea that this is the situation and that she has to focus on finding solutions to improve the child's mindset, which will allow him to have a healthy, balanced lifestyle and at the same time be at peace with himself and the Universe. Then she realizes how wrong she is... She just doesn't practice what she explains to others. She talks to them about vision, about faith moving mountains, about believing with all your being in something to happen and it is she, she... who gives such lessons to others, she doubts the appearance of a cure in the future. How hard it is often to understand a human mind! Or... how hard it is to do the things you know so well. It's not for nothing they say theory is one thing, but practice kills you... She wishes for a miracle cure just like Dad. What happens then? Why doesn't she believe with all her being that it really can happen? Who are you, woman, not to believe? Where do diseases come from? Exactly. That's where people come from. It's all God's will. Or Allah, or the Universe, or whatever everyone wants to call it. So what? If He allowed this in the child's life... If He allowed his grandmother to have cancer and be cured, to play with her grandchildren 7 years later, even though the doctors had given her very little time.... who are you, not to believe? How short-sighted we are sometimes.... Lately there's all the talk about the power of the mind, visualizations and successes or closed minds and repeated failures. That's exactly what any action we take is about. We need to think big, trust and feel like things have already happened. Be good people, pray and trust the Universe! You will have a surprise! A pleasant one.

26. VACATION PLANS: ALL-INCLUSIVE VERSUS SELF CATERING, POTS AND PANSTHE

The first vacation after the diagnosis was... postponed. A lot. They all felt the need to get away, to do new things, to take a break from everyday life. But unfortunately, they really couldn't decide how to proceed, or who to trust first. On the one hand they knew how serious the whole regime story was. On the other hand, they looked forward to relaxation, a holiday in the true sense of the word. On the internet forums, there are people who say they eat carelessly at restaurants, that they carefully explain to the waiter what to communicate to the kitchen, and rarely they have had any problems. On the other hand, there are those who claim that no celiac should do this, because the food is certainly contaminated if there is no separate preparation line. The question then, of course, would be: who is right? Well, in their own way, they may all be right. You can't argue with any of them. Especially since everyone is free to decide for himself. When you study the problem in more depth, the reality is that there are people whose body reacts immediately and very badly, with general discomfort, tiredness, abdominal cramps, changes in stools, vomiting and much more. But there are also people, even among those with celiac disease, who have no immediate reaction after accidentally becoming contaminated. But this does not mean that there are no reactions in the intestine. They are simply not noticed by the patient. And this is all the worse because, if this behaviour is maintained, it can lead over time to other problems. That is why it is best for everyone to choose for themselves, but only if they have thoroughly researched the matter and make an informed choice.

Choosing a holiday destination requires the greatest care and seriousness on everyone's part when there is a celiac in the family. You can't go away as spontaneously as you used to and not anywhere, anyway. Research needs to be done beforehand on the location, the region, and possibly the restaurants and supermarkets in the area if it's for a longer period of time. Because gluten-free products are not to be found everywhere, and it's not nice to find yourself without bread or biscuits for the kids on holiday. Erik's mom does some serious provisioning in this regard. She also prepares some cooked food for the road and for the first day of the holiday for both him and the baby. Since she has children, she's already used to doing this. Just as she's used to pampering herself on holiday with an early breakfast, hot tea and a strong dose of optimism about the day ahead. This time, everything was different. The first mistake was to choose an all-inclusive resort, fooling themselves that they would do better with meals for both adults and baby, as well as the celiac child. They would cook just for the little ones, but they would no longer have to take care of them. The details they left out, however, made all the difference... and they won't repeat this mistake in the future. The time they didn't cook for four wasn't for more fun and exploration, as they had originally intended, but to explain to the curious child, to wait on each other as they ate one at a time, more in secret, to work out the frustrations that came from the whole thing.

"Wow... so much food," Erik exclaimed as they passed the restaurant on their way to the pool. „I want to go there! Let's eat there! What's good?"

"Honey, you just ate in your room. Do you want to go play for a while, then we'll get ready for the beach?"

"Yeah, we can. But let's go for a little while, please. Just to see what they have!"

„Why do you want to do that? Please! You know they cook with gluten here. It's very crowded and I don't trust them to make us something uncontaminated. Come on, I'll get you some fruit if you like!"

"And go straight to the beach? I want in the water!"

"Okay," said Mom. „We'll do that. I'll talk to Daddy so I can go with you first."

"Well... aren't you eating?" said the man.

"No. Don't worry! Go and drink your coffee quietly, I don't

want to repeat the day before, when he analyzed every morsel on our plate. I couldn't even chew... even if I choose my gluten-free base, I'm afraid it might be contaminated in case he asks me for something. And if I offer him some of his casserole he doesn't want any... Never mind! I've got some nuts in my backpack, I'll get some more fruit and that's enough."

"As you wish! I'll be there as soon as I can. It wasn't such a good idea to come here, then. We'd rather spend this time together, preparing the meal, and then we could all have fun without any worries! He"s really small... in the future I suggest we still choose self-catering locations, in case we can"t find all inclusive gluten-free hotel. Even if we spend some time in the kitchen, at least we're sitting together and not creating frustration on either side. Anyway, no matter where we go we have all sorts of pots and pans with us, we are equipped and prepared for such situations."

"Yes. We'll see how we can manage..."

The woman thought it would never be the same again. It wasn't the food itself, nor the variety of assortments, the new dishes she'd get to taste, the flavour of the mouth-watering cakes present at every meal on the all-inclusive diet... It was more than that. It was about leisure, about freedom and choice, about experiences and relaxation, about not worrying about shopping for the next meal. All of that, however, was no longer an option. And as soon as everything was going to go a certain way in the future, they had to make a plan, find their own rhythm and organize themselves in such a way as to combine the useful with the pleasant. How were holidays going to be organized in the future so that everyone stayed healthy and peaceful? To first establish the new lifestyle, to complete the list of travel utensils needed for cooking, and to research healthy and tasty recipes that can be prepared quickly and do not require ingredients that cannot be safely transported or easily purchased near the accommodation. With a very clear plan and a little organisation, fun will be guaranteed. As she thought about all this, her mother's face lightened a little. It seemed as if things were beginning to settle down, slowly. After all, the problem wasn't the food. She had figured this out for some time, she had been aware of what was going on, but it was all so set in stone that she could hardly break away from all the habits she had been living with up until then. The problem really wasn't the food. The problem was in the way people had become accustomed to perceiving things, in which they believed there was joy, happiness.

She began to analyze the behaviour of those around her, and saw people eating at every step. Whenever, however and whatever. Some were standing in line for bagels, some for fast food, some for ice cream, some for popcorn... even at the beach their mouths were busy with boiled corn, ice cream, fruit, seeds or ice cocktails. She reflected on the times she had sat at the beach, lazily flipping through a book, and thinking about what else she could eat... in fact, it had never really been about "eating". It had always been more than that, and it was like she was blindfolded. It was always about something that needed to be filled in, something that was missing that could complete the picture of a perfect day, but not knowing where to look, people often looked for it in food. And they are pleased. But only for the moment. Because the void stays there for a long time. Sadly, many are unaware that the food they seek is food for the soul, not for the stomach. How easy it would have been if, at the beginning of the diet, someone had told her all this and had opened her eyes. Perhaps she would have looked at it differently, taken things more easily and not have acted as she did. If someone newly diagnosed were to ask her now about all this, she would tell her just that: "Forget everything you've learned so far! Forget your previous lifestyle, your old habits, forget everything and think! Meditate on the basic needs you have! Then think about how to satisfy them in the simplest and healthiest way possible. Without thinking about anyone and anything but your health and your goals! Exactly. You'll find that you get so obsessed with how, where and with whom you eat, that you forget all about your purpose on earth, your goals and your desires! That's what you need to work on. The rest... pure details". That's pretty much the conclusion she came to. And she still has so much to learn.

27. ERIK GOT INVITED TO A PARTY

After long late-night meditations and intense discussions with the little boy at bedtime, the parents have calmed down a little. Now they have a better plan for the holidays, everything is going well at home, things have settled down at kindergarten, the grandparents have got into the habit of the regime, so they can rest easy until the next challenge. And then it's not long before the child is invited to a birthday party. Great joy on the parents, who want to bring him along with other children of his age, but at the same time more frustration about the menu. What to do?The mother contacts the child's parents to find out the exact menu, so she can get the ingredients in advance and prepare the snacks, including the cake. On the day of the event, the mother organizes her diary according precisely to her schedule, because she has a lot to do. She has to bake pizzas and make cookies. To avoid what happened the other day, when the other kids argued over Erik's biscuits and he stood sulking in a corner because they asked him to give them to the other kids and they emptied his bag, she decided to bring a plate of gluten-free snacks so all the kids could eat. Of course, just like before any party, the parents are now preparing Erik, telling him again how things will go, what he can and can't do.

"Honey, you know we're going to the party. You're going to play nicely with the kids, you're going to give presents to the birthday boy, we're going to sing "Happy Birthday" together. and eat pizza and cake."

"Yay! And blow out the candles with him?"

"Well..., only he'll blow this time. You blew out the cake I made for your birthday. Did you forget?"

"No. But I still want to..."

"I imagine you do. Unfortunately, you can't. Look, you can blow on the cake I made you at home before we cut it. You know we have to take a piece back with us because they only have gluten cake there, right?"

"Yeah, they do. Let me blow now, I want to!"

Excited by the party atmosphere, Erik forgot about the conversation with his mother, and after the birthday boy blew out the candles, he "slipped" his hands in the hands of the other children, who had begun to "strip" the cake quickly from the decor.

"Baby, you know that it' s made with gluten! Don't take it, please!"

"But all the children took it. Please! Just one figure."

"They did, you're right. But it has gluten. Come on, be reasonable!"

"I know it does... but they're from my cartoons. I just want to keep it, that's all" he said softly, glaring at all the other kids munching on the hard marzipan.

The father nodded, patting him and kissing his head lovingly. He was proud of him. He had grown into a big boy: responsible, sociable and smart. He felt sorry for the situation he was in, but he knew that only by standing his ground, firmly, would he rescue the situation. They were fighting a long-term "war", and to win in the end he was obliged to serve his son all these refusals now. With regret for how it made him feel, but with joy for what keeping away gluten meant for his body. In the end, the important thing is that the child is well, that he feels well, that his body functions as well as possible and that he can have a beautiful and fulfilling life. Now, his every wish could be a challenge. And he has many, like any child who lives surrounded by challenges. Parents were used to that kind of line: "Shall we have some of that watermelon ice cream?"" Or: „I'd like one of those biscuits... do we have anything to eat?"

But after taking an inventory of the last few months, they concluded that the healthiest thing to do was to explain why he was allowed something and justify it with understandable arguments when he refused something. Because refusals are many, and not just about what he is allowed, but how much of something he is allowed to. Of course, by trying all sorts of gluten-free sweets, the child has come to have favourites among them too. And he would eat crackers and jelly beans all day long.

'I'm afraid that, in our desire to try to replace old products, we might somehow abuse similar gluten-free products, which in many cases are even sweeter and not healthy. Many people seem to fall into this trap. And "gluten-free" doesn't necessarily mean organic or healthier. I didn't realize what that meant at first when my doctor explained it to me, but now I understand perfectly. Besides bread, which we usually make at home anyway, it's best to only occasionally eat commercial gluten-free baked goods. Erik has a weakness for some cookies that I find extremely sweet. We need to take action, and in order not to turn him away, it's best not to buy them at all, so he doesn't see them in the house. Because the other day he got very upset when I refused him, because he had already received one as a snack from the kindergarten. And he said something like: "When I get big and you get small, I'll do the same to you..." and it's not the first time he'd said that to me. He's also said it to me when I raised my voice at him after he pushed Dodo or in other contexts. So, my opinion is that we need to sit down again and agree on how to proceed with him. After all, the fact that he's on a diet and not being allowed certain foods shouldn't make him either spoiled or naughty or frustrated. He simply needs to learn that, precisely BECAUSE of this diet, he has a chance at a normal, healthy life. And first of all, this should be ingrained in our minds. It took us a long time to understand something the doctor told us from day one, but you know what they say: better late than never. And I also believe that no matter what anyone tells you, until you convince yourself of that, until you go through certain steps to draw your own conclusions, you hardly convince yourself of anything. That's why it's best for everyone to experiment and decide for themselves. Until Erik grows up a little more, however, we are responsible for his education and healthy and harmonious growth, so I hope we make the best decisions for him.'

ABOUT THE AUTHOR

Finally, we have reached the end and you may be wondering who I am? Nothing is harder than writing about myself. I've been working as an editor since university. I also "tested out" as a teacher for a very short time, alongside being a journalist, only to realize that although I love working with children, I love writing more and more.

In my 10+ years in journalism and a few years in public relations, I've had the idea several times to create a blog, where I could put my thoughts, but this only came to life after I had my second child. That was when I was writing the last pages of the memory book I had started when I delivered my first son. And as more and more people asked me how we were doing in the formula of 4, I thought maybe it would be helpful to leave my notes out for others to see. And that way I'd have access to our memories, too, when I wanted to. That's how www.tagarta.ro has started, a soul project that is just at the beginning.

After creating the site and posting the first articles, I felt a huge desire for personal development. And once I started on this journey, I told myself that it is not enough to keep only for myself the precious information that I discover day by day and that turns out to be transformational. So, in my free time, I am sharing my knowledge and journey with readers.

I know exactly what it feels like to lose track of things, to no longer be in control of your life, to have your decisions influenced by those around you, and your own time no longer belonging to you. Two more years of "staying" at home just to take care of the little ones, cook for them every day and dress them in ironed striped bodysuits, without doing something for myself would have been time wasted. So I started looking... I didn't know exactly what I was looking for either, but my fantasies quickly materialized and all sorts of people and opportunities appeared in my life. And with the boy's illness I learned that we should be grateful and thank God for what we are and what we have and that no day should go by without learning something. Whether it's reading a book, taking a course, listening to a great material, sitting down with a mentor, or simply being quieter and listening to what others have to say. Because we have a lot to learn even from the little ones. Let's judge less, and at the end of each day remember to be grateful for simply BEING.

I hope our story will be an inspiration to you all!

Sincerely,
Catalina Tagarta

CLAIM YOUR **FREE BONUS**

I hope you enjoyed our story and that you have noted at least a few ideas that might help you to become a better parent and raise healthy, wise children.

I've also prepared a surprise for you: a free and **extremely valuable** <u>Time Management Guide</u> that will help you work on growing your dreams, but at the same time taking care of your kids and other daily duties.

All you have to do to receive the **FREE Guide** is to send me an **e-mail** at: contact.tagarta@gmail.com, with the **subject**: "Claim your free bonus".

By the way: I'm a beginning writer, so your feedback is very important to me. Please let me know how you found the book and if there is anything I could improve.

Good luck in everything you do and remember: **learning never ends**! We keep growing with our children!

Greetings,
Catalina

www.ingramcontent.com/pod-product-compliance
Lightning Source LLC
LaVergne TN
LVHW050645200726
843506LV00010B/1378